Nuffield Maths

CHALLENGERS C
ENCOUNTERS WITH SHAPE
Teachers' Handbook

Authors

John Hargreaves
Formerly Warden of Morpeth Teachers' Centre, Northumberland
Ron Wyvill
Formerly Headteacher, Huish County Primary School, Yeovil

Contents

D1808992

Nuffield Maths

General editor: Eric A Albany

Teachers' notes and answers

Introduction

Challengers C (Encounters with Shape) concentrates on many of the spatial ideas that most children of 11 or 12 years old will have met already. In some cases, topics met earlier are extended. For example, the chapters on polyshapes widen the study of polyominoes to include hexominoes and then to investigate what happens if, instead of squares, equilateral triangles, right-angled triangles or trapezia are used as starting motifs. Also, problems and investigations involving several different types of tangram are introduced.

Measurement, estimation and approximation all play an important part and recording is facilitated by using isometric or lattice grid paper. (Master sheets for photocopying are at the back of this book.)

Much of the work is of a practical nature – encouraging children to learn by manipulating two-dimensional shapes cut out or made from elastic bands on pinboards, and three-dimensional shapes folded from nets, built from interlocking cubes or constructed in skeletal form.

To quote from paragraph 292 of *Mathematics Counts*, the Report of the Cockcroft Committee:

> *Almost all children find pleasure in working with shapes, and work of this kind can encourage the development of positive attitudes towards mathematics in those finding difficulty with number work. The rich variety of practical work which is possible in the primary years provides a foundation on which the more formal geometry of the secondary years can be based.*

Elizabeth Williams and Hilary Shuard in *Primary Mathematics Today* make the point:

> *Different kinds of manipulation of shapes involve some operations which are common to all kinds of mathematical activity: sorting, combining, partitioning, matching, ordering and fundamental types of movement.*
> *Practical experience of spatial relationships is one of the foundations on which other mathematical relationships and operations can be built.*

The authors, John Hargreaves and Ron Wyvill, have called upon their vast experience of primary school mathematics to produce a wealth of fascinating and challenging material for children to benefit from and enjoy.

ERIC A. ALBANY
General editor

Solids from nets

Paper-folding has always been a favourite pastime for children of all ages. Each generation proceeds through a succession of darts, aeroplanes, boats and hats, all made from whatever scraps of paper are to hand. The traditional designs call for no prior drawing; the cutting (or more likely, tearing) and folding are usually approximate. This cavalier approach is all very well for simple symmetrical models but greater care becomes more necessary for more precise structures.

Three guiding principles are applied in making mathematical models.

i Accurate drawing is of prime importance. A two-dimensional drawing, referred to as a *net*, embodies all the information needed for producing a given three-dimensional shape.

ii Cutting must follow carefully the lines of the net. Scissors are usually adequate and safer, though greater precision may be obtained by using a sharp knife, a metal safety rule and a cutting board.

iii All the lines of the net are intended to be either cut or folded. Folding, like cutting, must always be exactly along the drawn line. To ensure this, scoring first is essential. After scoring, a line almost folds itself between finger and thumb; then further pressure by the thumb nail results in a sharp, clean crease.

1 It is intended that pupils visualise each net being folded or rolled into its appropriate three-dimensional shape. The completed table should read:

Net letter	Shape number	Name of shape
A	2	Open box
B	1	Open cone
C	4	Open cylinder
D	5	Open cone
E	3	Tetrahedron

The open cone appears twice. The net of an open cone is a sector of a circle; the greater the sector angle, the flatter the cone.

2 Of the five nets, the only example of a closed shape is the tetrahedron. The other four become fully enclosed if the box is given an additional square and the cylinder a circle at each end, while the cones each need a circle.

After completing the table, pupils should draw each net on suitable paper (cartridge or thin card) ready for cutting out. Each fold line must be carefully scored. This may be done by ballpoint pen and ruler, but if thicker card is used for more permanent models, the scoring may need a light knife-stroke.

The reverse process of building a solid from a net is that of opening out an existing three-dimensional shape such as a chocolate box tray so that it is returned to its original flat shape. Collecting a variety of cartons or packages and displaying their flattened nets makes a useful class activity.

3 All solids with triangular faces and a base of three or more sides are called pyramids. A pyramid with a triangular base is called a *tetrahedron* from the Greek *tetra*, 'four'; *hedron*, 'face'.

4 In addition to the two pentominoes shown, there are six more which fold into an open box:

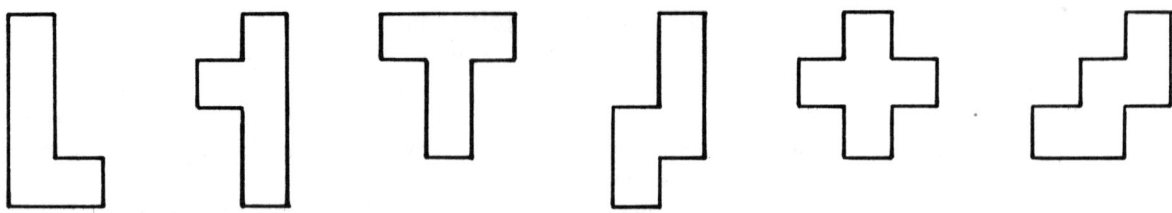

5 Of the 35 hexominoes there are eleven which fold to make a closed cube:

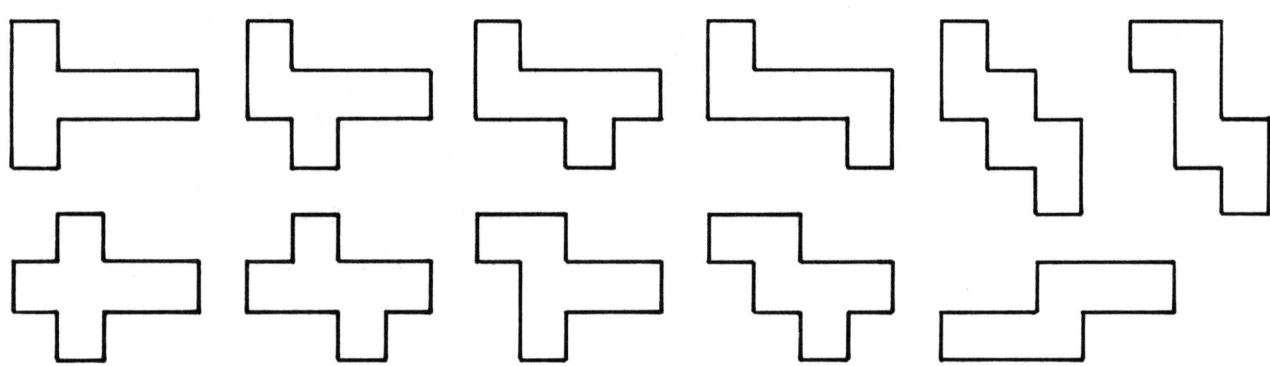

The net for a cuboid has this general form.

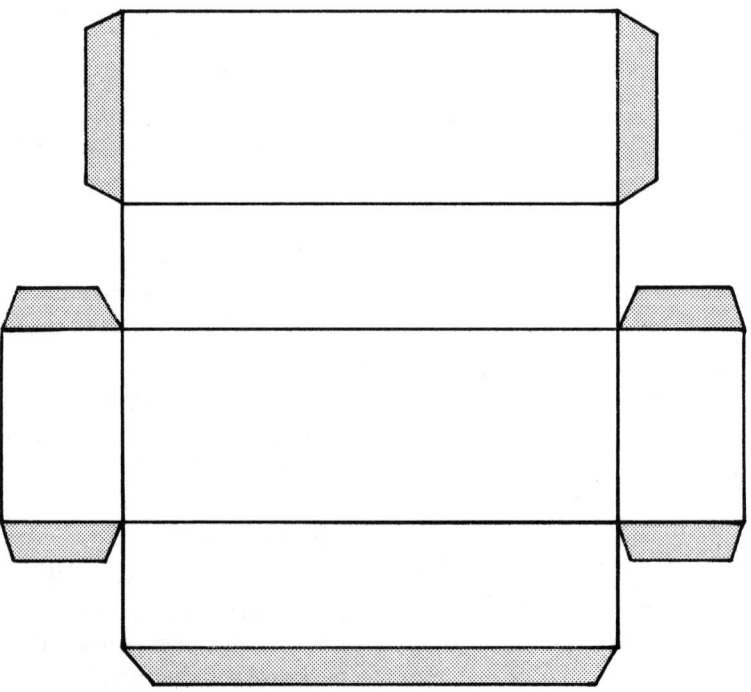

6 A prism is described according to the shape of its end (or cross-section).

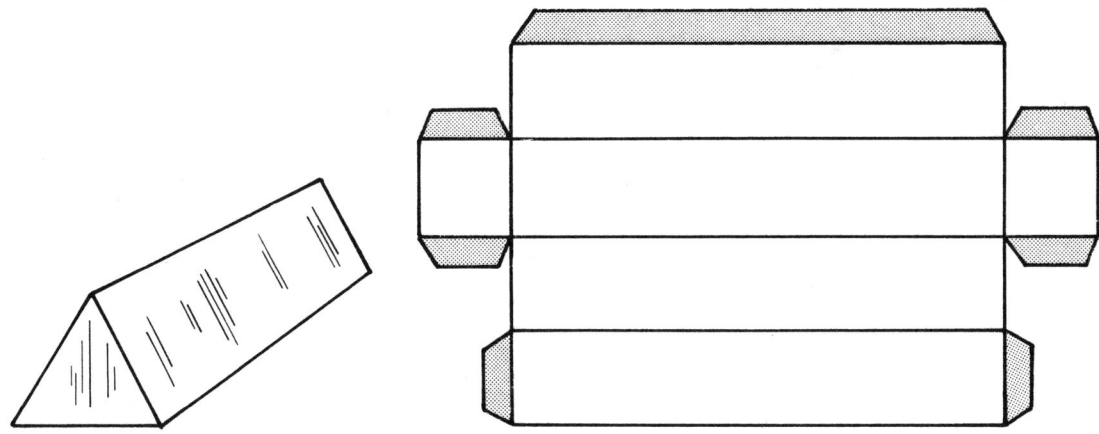

A sketch of a triangular prism   A net for a square prism

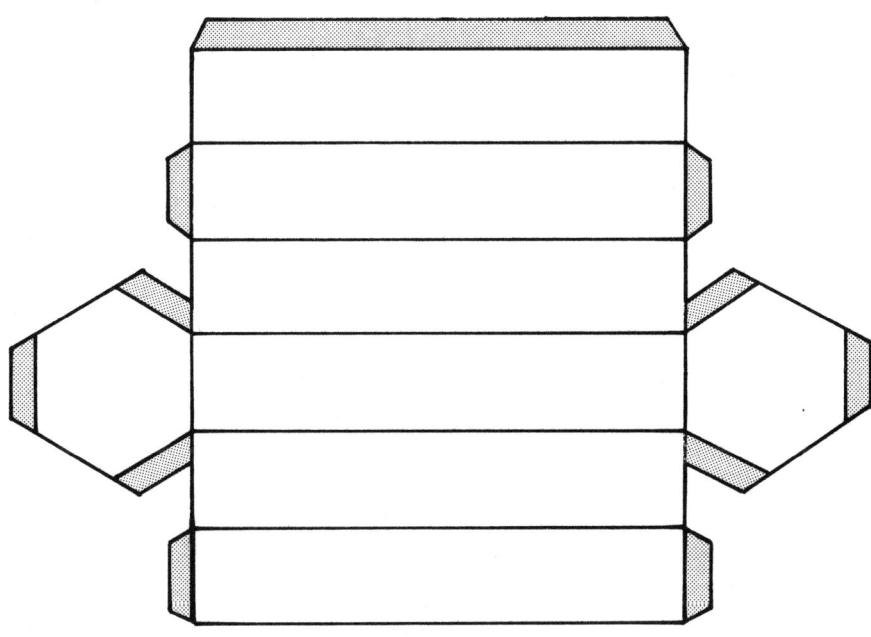

A net for a hexagonal prism

7 A pyramid is named according to the shape of its base.

The Pyramids of Egypt have a square base and four triangular faces.

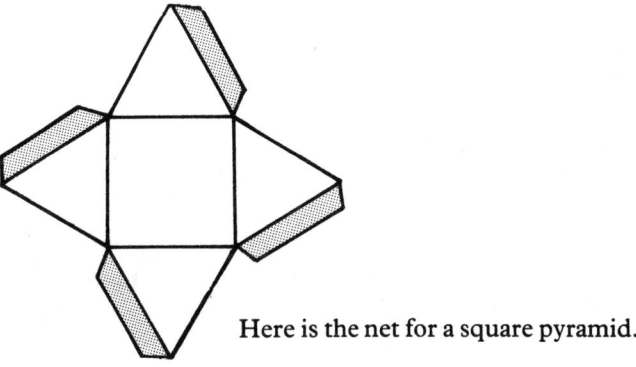

Here is the net for a square pyramid.

The net for a hexagonal pyramid consists of a central hexagon and six triangles.

8 The importance of scoring a fold has already been stressed. A *reverse fold*, scored on the *back* of the net, is introduced in the desk calendar.

Folds are of two kinds:

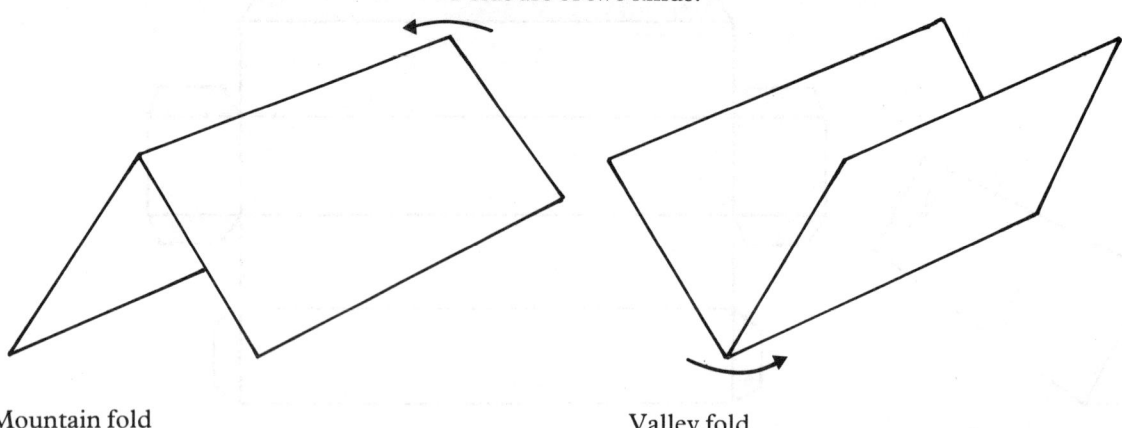

Mountain fold   Valley fold

By convention they are indicated in the drawing by different kinds of broken lines:

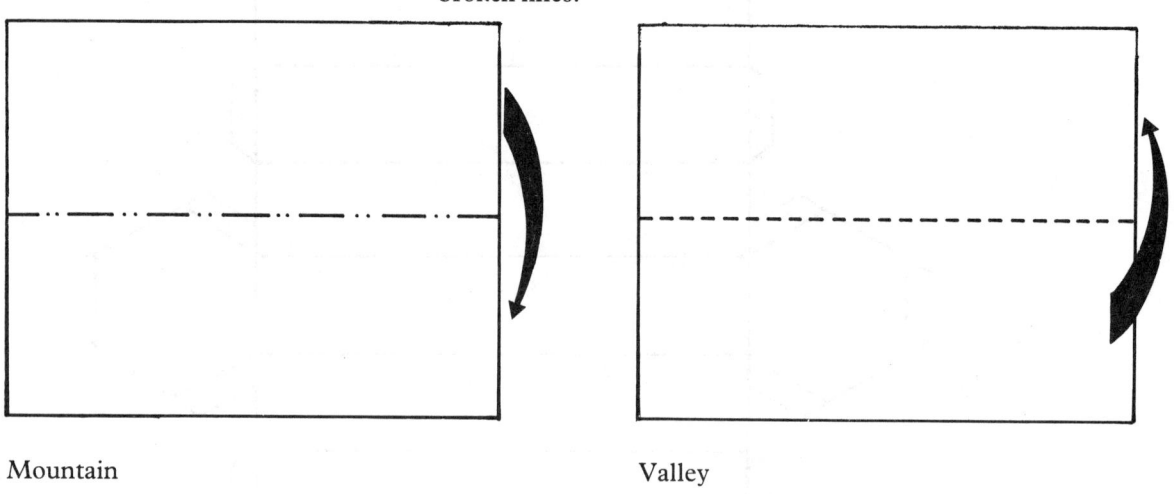

Mountain   Valley

Both types may be encountered in the one net. For example, a drawing marked as A below would be folded as in sketch B.

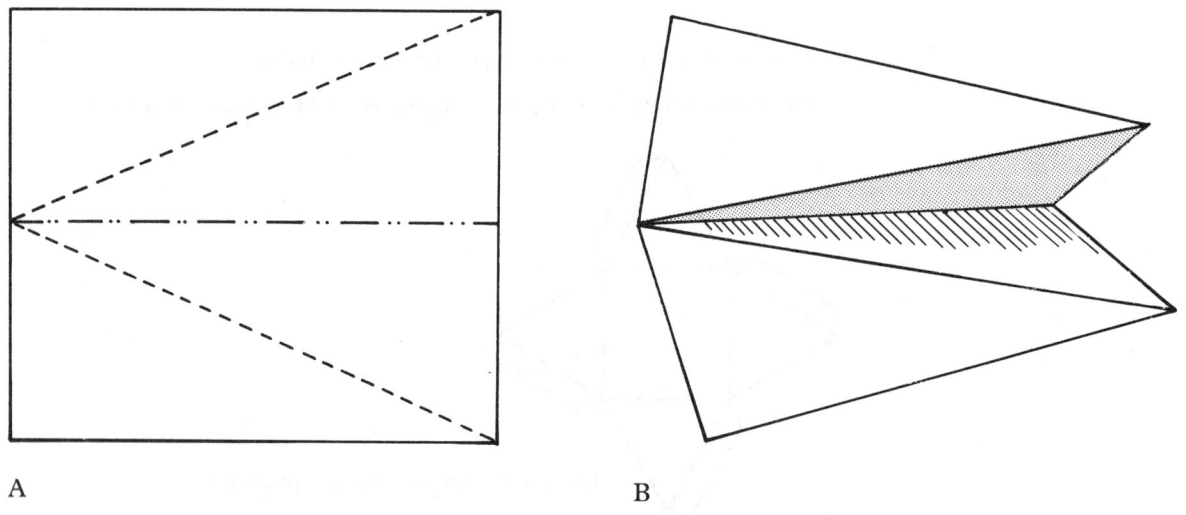

A   B

The centre-fold is scored on the front of the card and the two diagonal folds are scored on the reverse.

A more difficult exercise using reverse folding is provided by the pentagram: the five-pointed Star of Bethlehem.

Paste it onto card for a wall display or, alternatively, glue two pentagrams back to back for a hanging decoration. The prominence of the star is increased if the background triangles (labelled 'B') are coloured.

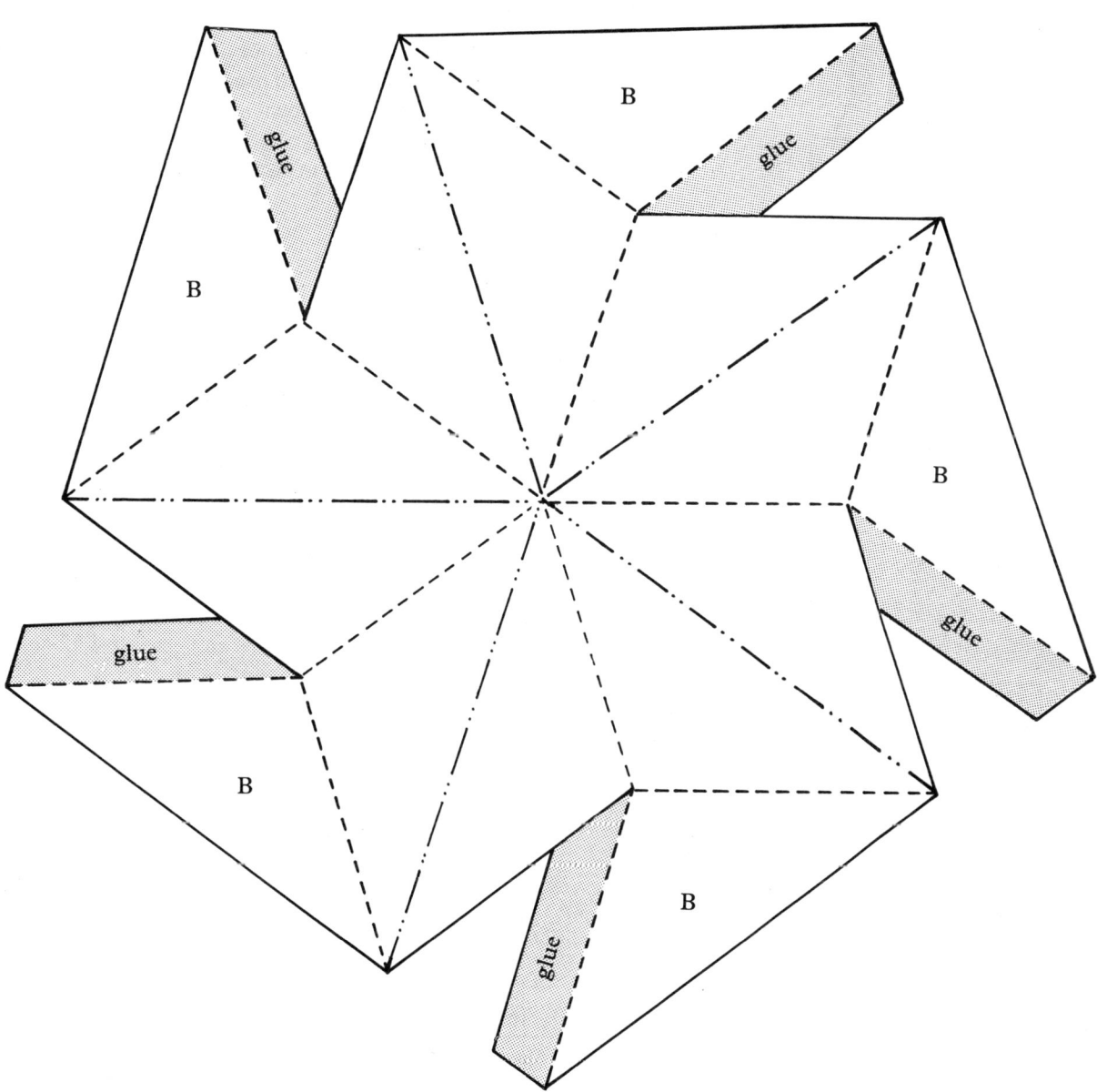

This chapter starts with a brief revision of work on the polyominoes formed from one to five squares: that is, monominoes, dominoes, trominoes, tetrominoes and pentominoes. More detailed information on these can be found in Chapter 10 of *Nuffield Maths 6 Teachers' Handbook*.

The set of distinct *hexominoes* can be produced by adding a single square (monomino) to each of the twelve pentominoes in as many ways as possible. Finding the complete set of 35 hexominoes is a useful class or group activity which provides points for discussion about the duplications occurring from rotation and reflection.

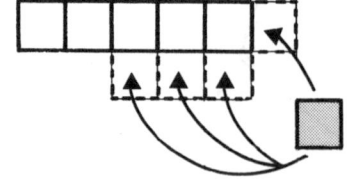

1 a Using a straight pentomino, there are four possible positions for the monomino. The other positions would produce duplications.

  b The four distinct hexominoes are shown in the table below for question **2**.

  c Two of these four hexominoes are symmetrical. (See table below.)

2

Shape	Area in square units	Perimeter in units	Number of joined edges	Number of axes of symmetry
	6	14	5	2
	6	14	5	0
	6	14	5	0
	6	14	5	1

This table may lead pupils to think that all hexominoes have the same area of six square units and the same perimeter. However, the next table (for question **3**) shows that it is possible for shapes to have the same area but *different* perimeters.

Some children may wish to investigate the possible connection between the perimeter and the number of joined sides. (This is dealt with on page 64 of *Nuffield Maths 6 Teachers' Book*.)

3

Shape	Area in square units	Perimeter in units	Number of joined edges	Number of axes of symmetry
	6	12	6	0
	6	14	5	0
	6	14	5	1
	6	14	5	0
	6	14	5	0
	6	14	5	0
	6	14	5	1
	6	14	5	0
	6	14	5	0
Shape	Area in square units	Perimeter in units	Number of joined edges	Number of axes of symmetry

4 The complete set of 35 hexominoes is shown below. The order in which pupils find them will depend upon their choice of a starting pentomino from which to generate the hexominoes by trying all the possible ways of adding a monomino. Encourage pupils to do this in a systematic way, rejecting duplicates as they go.

5 The hexominoes are divided into *odd* and *even*; that is, those which have three shaded squares when placed on a chessboard and those which have either two or four shaded squares. In the case of pentominoes, the number of shaded squares can either be two or three depending on how the pentomino is placed on the chessboard, so it is not possible to classify them as odd or even.

Polyshapes 1   Pupils' Book page 6

The hexominoes are also partitioned to show those with/without line symmetry (questions **6** and **7**) and those which will/will not fold to make a cube (question **8**). Hexominoes with rotational symmetry are marked with an asterisk *.

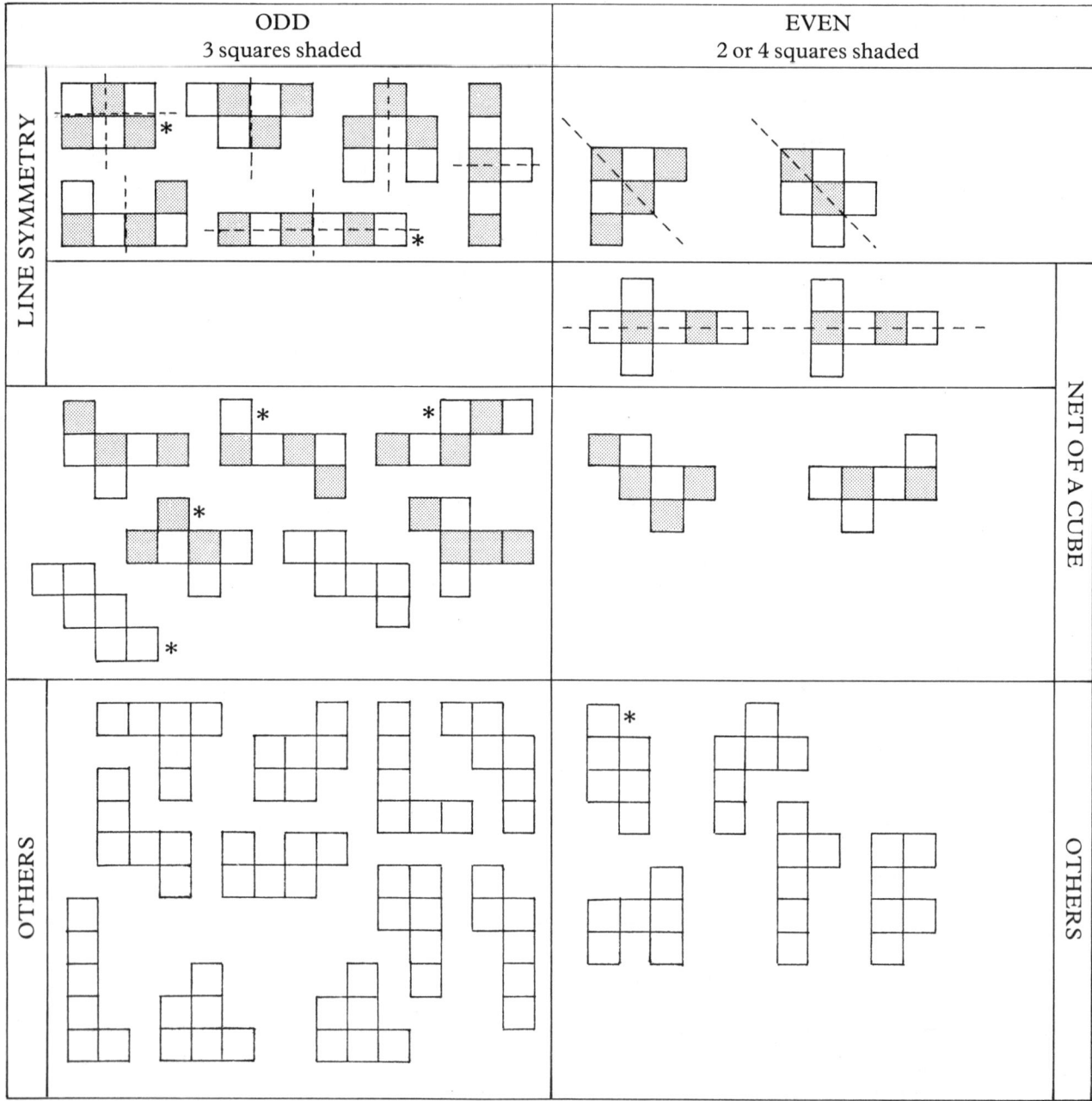

9 (These are not necessarily the only solutions.)

a

b

c

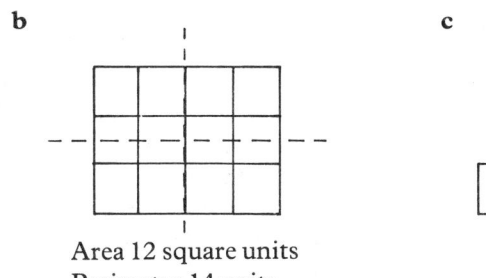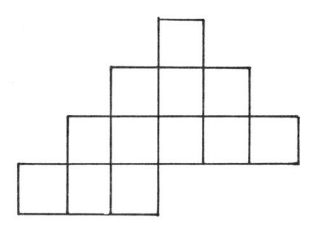

Area 12 square units
Perimeter 18 units

Area 12 square units
Perimeter 14 units

Area 12 square units
Perimeter 20 units

If the number of identical pieces is extended to four, many interesting patterns are possible. Such experimentation should be encouraged.

Polyshapes 1   **Pupils' Book page 7**

10 b Four axes of symmetry (horizontal, vertical and two diagonal).
  c Area is 24 square units and perimeter is 24 units.
  d Four times.

11 (These are not necessarily the only possible solutions.)

One axis of symmetry

Two axes of symmetry

Not symmetrical

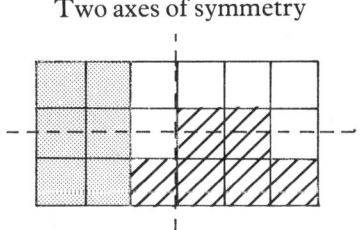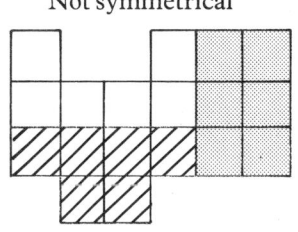

Area 18 square units
Perimeter 20 units

Area 18 square units
Perimeter 18 units

Area 18 square units
Perimeter 22 units

12 (These are not necessarily the only possible solutions.)

One axis of symmetry

Two axes of symmetry

Not symmetrical

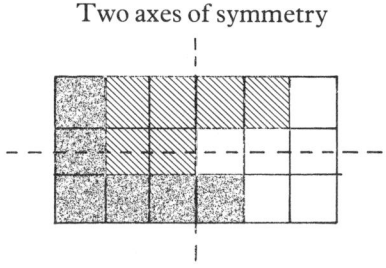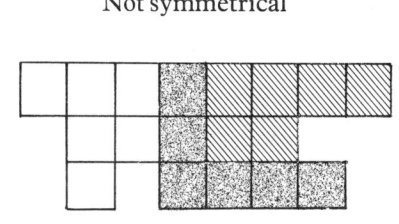

Area 18 square units
Perimeter 26 units

Area 18 square units
Perimeter 18 units

Area 18 square units
Perimeter 26 units

These activities emphasise yet again that shapes with the same area do not necessarily have the same perimeter.

Drawing solid shapes 1

Isometric projection is a method of drawing much used by engineering draughtsmen because it has the dual advantage of a pictorial view and trueness of dimension. (Greek: *iso*, 'equal'; *metron*, 'measure'.)

The three perpendicular axes of a solid are represented by the three lines on isometric paper – one vertical and the other two making angles of 30° with the horizontal ground line. Different sizes of isometric grid paper are available, though 1 cm (distance between vertices) is the most useful for present purposes. An alternative to continuous lines is in the form of a dotted grid which can be used by pupils when they are sufficiently experienced.

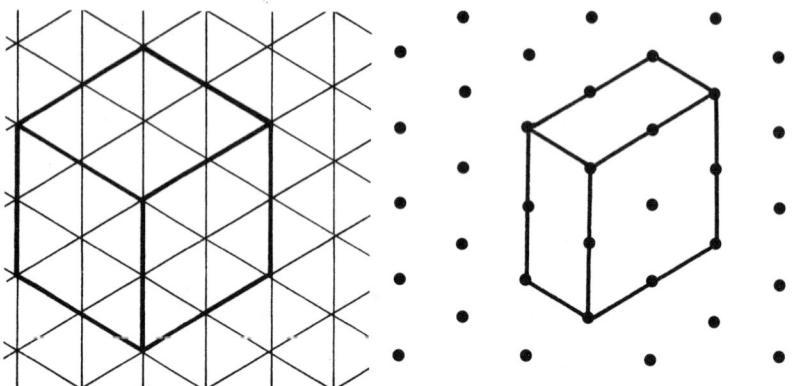

A photograph and an artist's sketch both differ from an isometric drawing because they show the appearance of a solid from a fixed viewpoint.

Vertical lines appear in their true upright position, but horizontal lines, though actually parallel, appear to converge toward a vanishing point on the horizon.

In perspective drawing the rectangular side elevations are shown as trapezia, whereas in isometric drawing they become parallelograms.

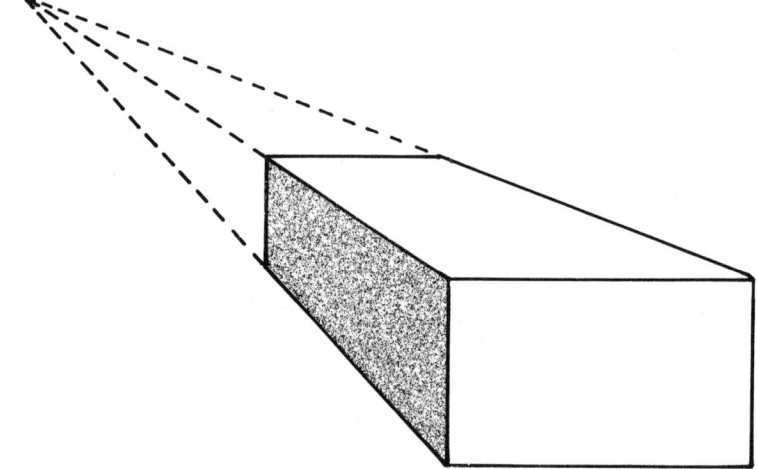

The solids portrayed in the *Pupils' Book* can all be represented by lines drawn over the existing grid lines or by joining adjacent dots on a dotted grid.

1 Centicube or other types of plastic interlocking cubes are useful for making the solid models represented by the drawings. The sockets and nebs, necessary for joining, are ignored in drawing.

2 The volume of A is 1 cubic unit; B is 2 cubic units; C and D are each 8 cubic units. A and C are the cubes.

3 Three faces are shown; three are hidden.

4 These are solid pentominoes. The set of solid pentominoes is limited to twelve planar figures; that is, those in which all five cubes lie in one plane. These correspond to the twelve two-dimensional pentominoes show on page 4 of the *Pupils' Book*. The total number of solids which can be formed by joining five cubes (not necessarily in the same plane) is stated by Solomon Golomb to be 29. Finding some or all of them could lead to a challenging group investigation.

5 Here are two views, one in combination and the other exploded, of one possibility for joining a third pentomino to the two given.

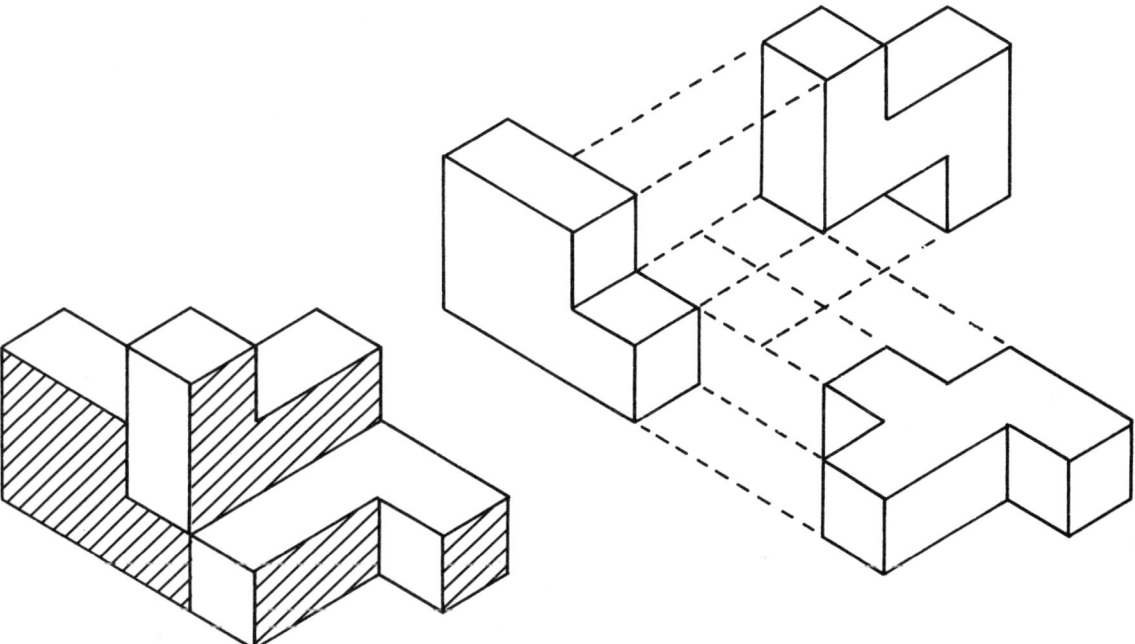

Two pentominoes joined together have a volume of 10 cubic units; three have a volume of 15 cubic units and twelve have a volume of 60 cubic units.

Pinboards, or geoboards, provide excellent opportunities to explore and develop, in a tangible way, many interesting concepts associated with two-dimensional shape. Shapes can be formed quickly and easily without the need for accurate drawing and measuring by using elastic bands stretched around the pins. For early experiences a 3 by 3 pinboard is quite adequate.

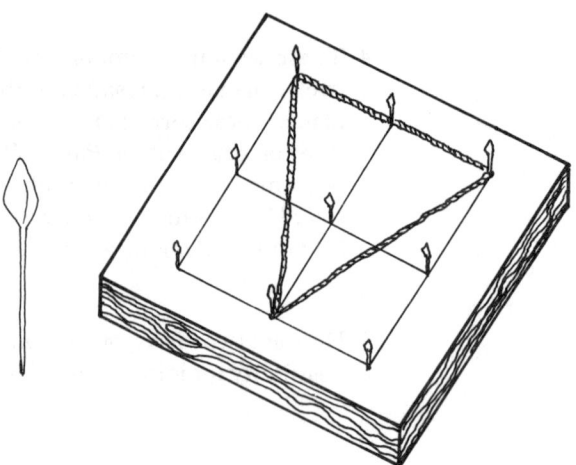

Pinboards can be made using offcuts of wood large enough to allow the pins to be spaced at least two centimetres apart with a border of at least one centimetre. Smooth-headed panel pins or hardboard pins are the best types to use as they do not have sharp edges on which fingers or elastic bands may be damaged.

Ideally, elastic bands of different colours and lengths should be available. Recording is simplified by providing dot lattice paper or specially prepared sheets. (A master sheet for photocopying is included in this book.) Areas are expressed in 'square units' and lengths in 'units'.

Initially, there should be a reasonable amount of time allowed for free experimentation in forming shapes or designs which could be copied, either freehand or by using a ruler, on to centimetre-squared or dot lattice paper. Even on a 3 by 3 board there are many possibilities. Here are a few:

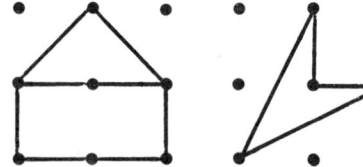 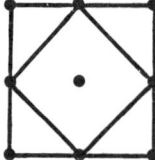 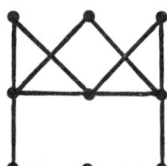 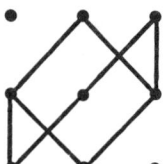 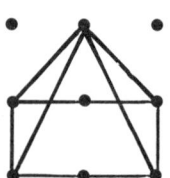

1 Children should be encouraged to talk about the shapes they have made and compare results. Within these early shapes and designs many of the common two-dimensional shapes will be seen and this is a natural lead into the more formal work which follows. Teacher-pupil discussion, building up useful vocabulary, is essential at this stage and is aided if a large demonstration pinboard is displayed with shirring elastic or string replacing the elastic bands.

2 a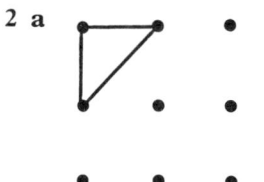

   b Right-angled isosceles

c Yes

d Here are some of the sixteen possible positions.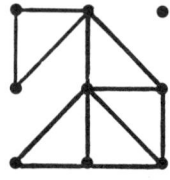

e Half a square unit

3 and **4**

Shape	A	B	C	D	E	F	G	H	I	J	K	L	M	N	O
Area (sq. units)	4	1	$\frac{1}{2}$	$3\frac{1}{2}$	3	$2\frac{1}{2}$	2	2	2	1	3	2	2	$2\frac{1}{2}$	$\frac{1}{2}$
Perimeter (units)	8	4	3·4	7·4	6·8	6·2	13·6	5·6	6	5·2	7·2	6·4	6·4	6·6	4·6

5 a There are sixteen ways.

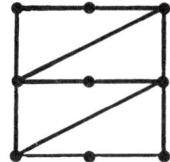 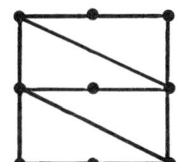 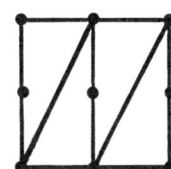 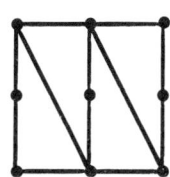

b 1 square unit   **c** 5 units (5·2)   **d** A right-angled scalene triangle

6 a

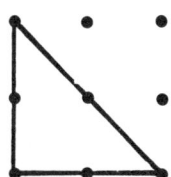   **b** 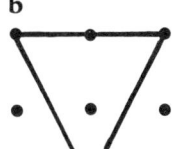 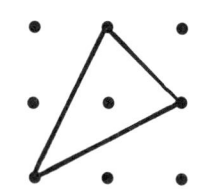   **c**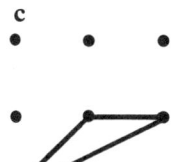

d Area   2 square units   2 square units $1\frac{1}{2}$ square units $\frac{1}{2}$ square unit
     Perimeter   1·8 units   6·4 units   5·8 units   4·6 units

7 a

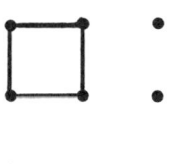   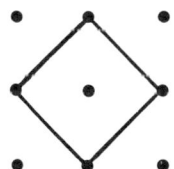   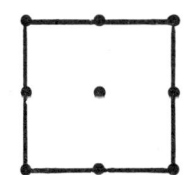

b   1 square unit   2 square units   4 square units

c   4 units   5·6 units   8 units

d a quarter   **e** a half   **f** a half

g As the perimeters of the squares double, the areas become four times as large. The perimeter of each square is four times the square root of its area.

8 a

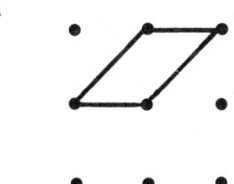   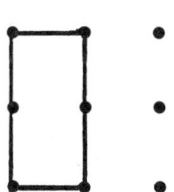   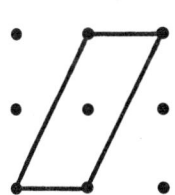

b Area   1 square unit   2 square units   2 square units
     Perimeter   4·8 units   6 units   6·4 units

8 c 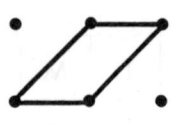 Area   1 square unit
Perimeter   4·8 units

d All with area of 1 square unit:

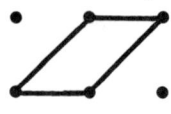 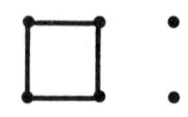 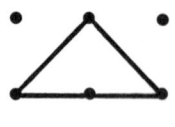

All with area of 2 square units:

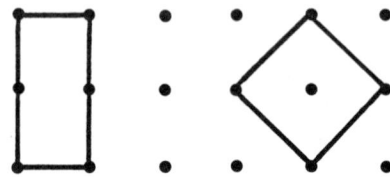 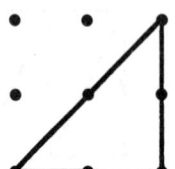  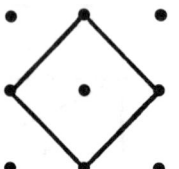 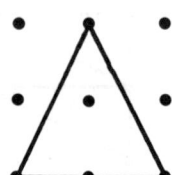

Pinboard Activities 1   Pupils' Book page 13

9 a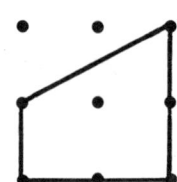

b 3 square units
c 7 units (7·2)

d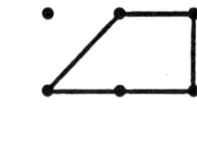

e 5·4 units

f Yes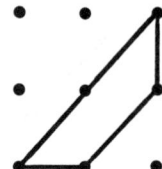

10 a 3 square units
b 6·8 units

c 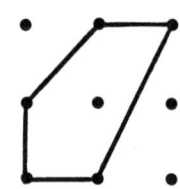   **d**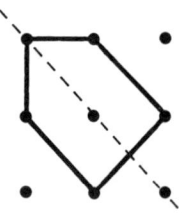

11 a A: 3 square units   B: 2 square units   C: 2½ square units
b A: 6·8 units   B: 8 units   C: 8·2 units

c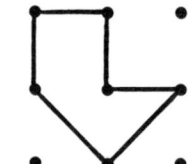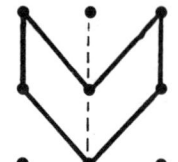

d Area 2 square units
Perimeter 6·8 units

Area 2 square units
Perimeter 7·6 units

Alternative asymmetrical hexagons:

2 square units
7·6 units

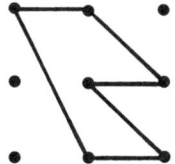

2 square units
8 units

2 square units
8 units

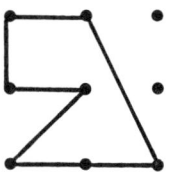

2½ square units
8·6 units

More Tangrams 1   Pupils' Book page 14

Most people consider the tangram as a form of puzzle with geometrical implications. However, it is quite likely that tangrams were originally designed as a means of instruction rather than as a pastime. This chapter and 'More Tangrams 2' are chiefly concerned with the former aspect. It is probably about 4000 years since the tangram was invented and over the years the instructional aspect appears to have been sacrificed in favour of the more flippant 'doodle' possibilities.

There are two versions of the original tangram. The one most commonly used (Tangram A) consists of a square dissected into five isosceles right-angled triangles, one square and one parallelogram. The seven pieces could be arranged to form two equal squares or a wide and varied range of representational shapes such as animals, birds, people, etc. (See *Challengers A*.)

In the other version of the original tangram (Tangram B), the square is dissected into four isosceles right-angled triangles, two squares and one parallelogram.

Squared card (centimetre-grid) is suggested as the best sort of material to use, but if this is not available, centimetre-squared paper could be glued firmly on to card.

In both figures the pieces are numbered and will be referred to as A1, A5, B7, etc. To save confusion in identification during discussion, it is important that every child numbers the pieces in the same way.

Each tangram is based on a square of side 10 centimetres, giving an area of 100 square centimetres. Opportunities will arise where simple formulae may be used in the solution of area problems:

Area of a square = length × breadth
Area of a triangle = ½(base × perpendicular height)
Area of a parallelogram = base × perpendicular height.

Also, Pythagoras' Theorem could be used to calculate the lengths of sides but, more usually, these are measured to the nearest centimetre. The square root of 200, for example, is very close to 14, and the square root of 50 is very close to 7. In these examples 14 cm and 7 cm would be used in exercises involving perimeters.

Note: In some cases pieces may be turned over in order to make the desired shape.

Tangram A

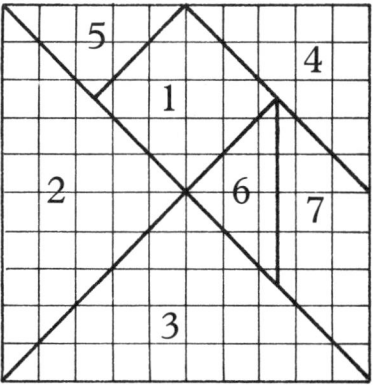

Tangram B

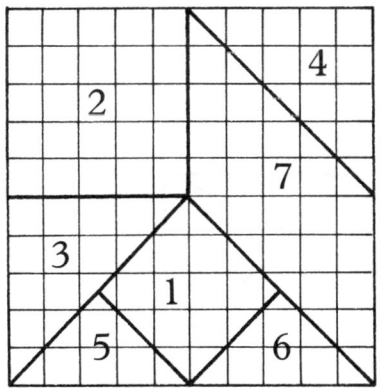

1 a   25 cm²
  b   Yes
  c   Yes
  d   Yes

1 e Either: count squares in B2 and squares and half-squares in B7 to show 25 square centimetres in each shape,

or: note that the parallelogram B7 can be cut into two identical right-angled isosceles triangles which could be superimposed on the square B2 to cover it exactly,

or: cut the square B2 along a diagonal and place the two triangles on the parallelogram B7 to cover it exactly.

f A3 is a quarter of the area of B5.   **i** One-eighth
g Yes   **j** B3 and B4
h B2, B3, B5, B6   **k** A5, A6, B5, B6

Tangram C consists of one square and four identical right-angled triangles.

Tangram C

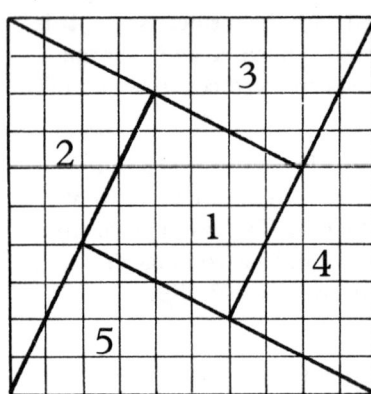

2 a

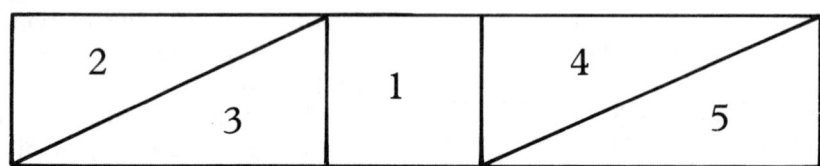

b Perimeter is 54 cm.

c

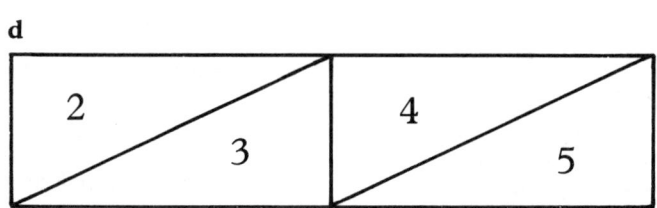

d

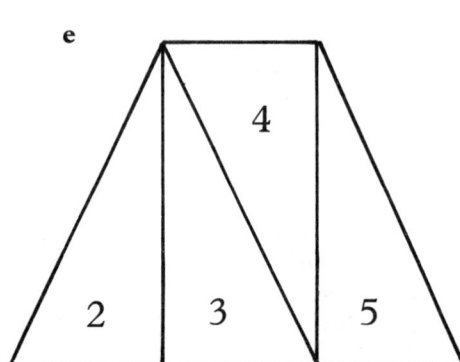

e

f Area $= \dfrac{9(13 \cdot 5 + 4 \cdot 5)}{2}$

$= \dfrac{9(18)}{2}$

$= 81 \text{ cm}^2$

More Tangrams 1

3 a

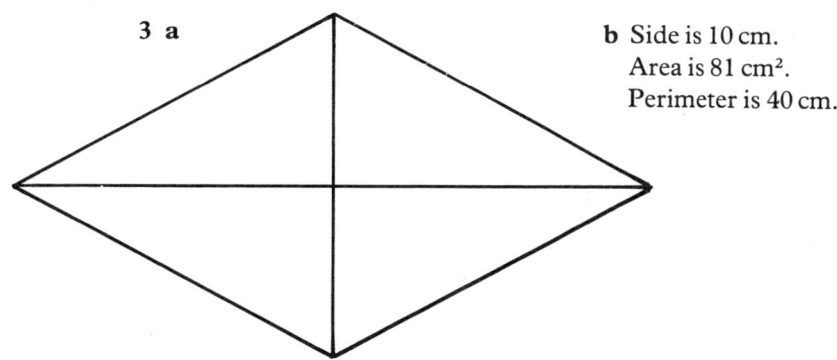

b Side is 10 cm.
Area is 81 cm^2.
Perimeter is 40 cm.

3 c and d There are several alternatives, all with an area of 100 cm^2. The approximate perimeters are marked beneath each diagram.

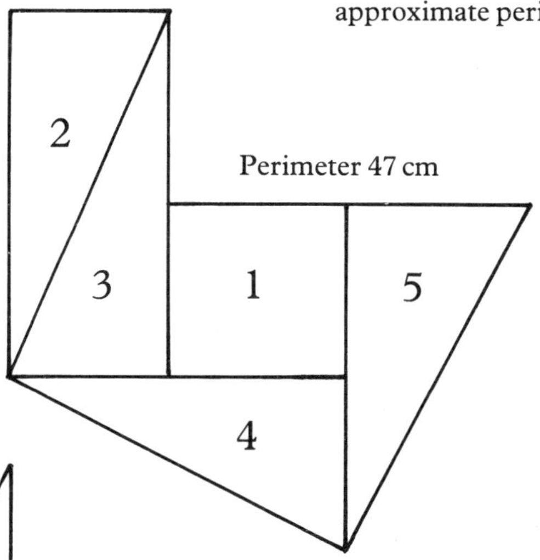

Perimeter 47 cm

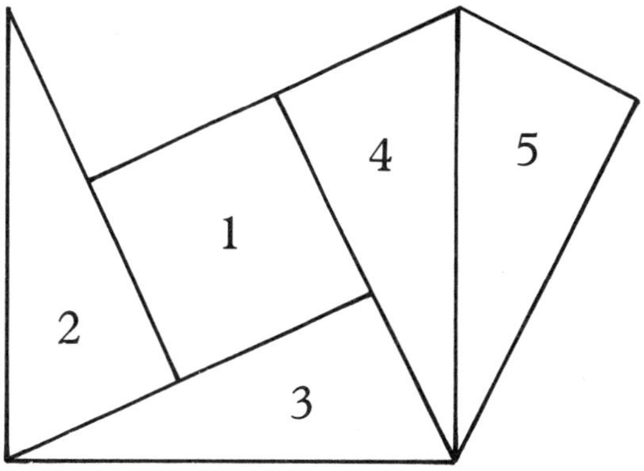

Perimeter 47 cm

Perimeter 47 cm

Perimeter 49 cm

Tangram D

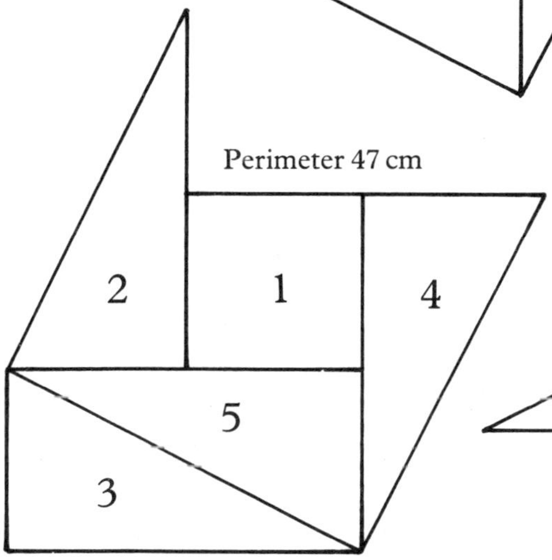

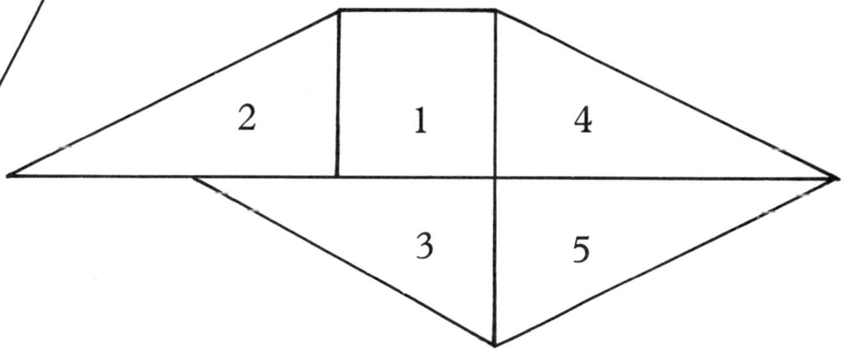

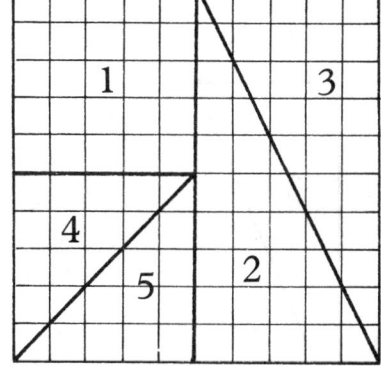

4 Tangram D consists of one square and four right-angled triangles – two large and two smaller ones which are also isosceles.

a Same
b Half
c Same
d Twice
e 50 cm^2

5 a

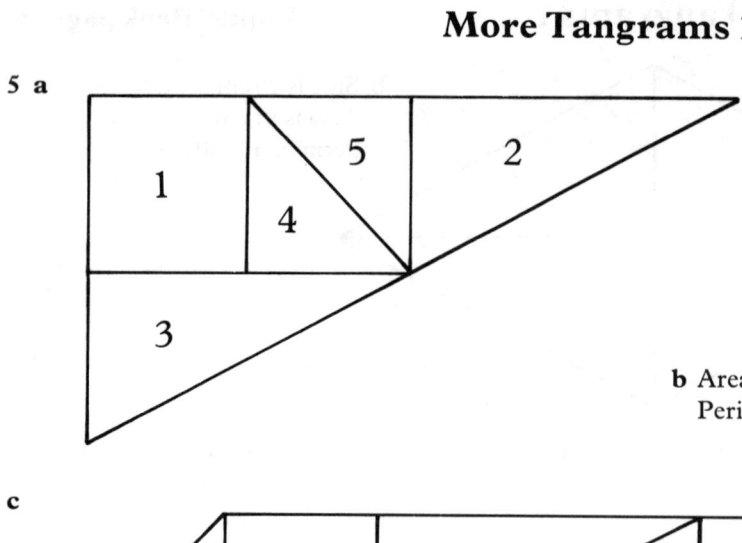

b Area is 100 cm².
   Perimeter is approximately 52 cm.

c

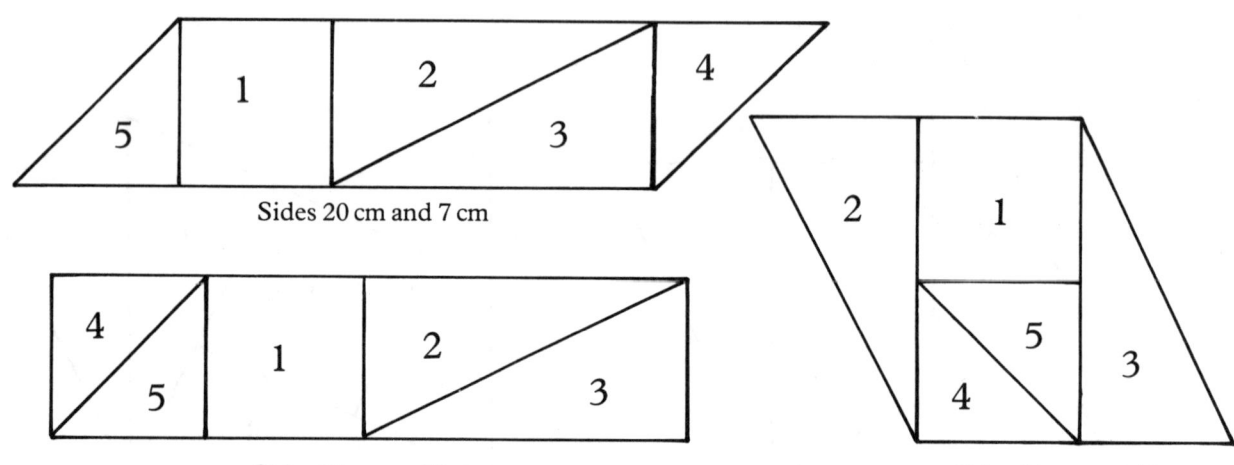

Sides 20 cm and 7 cm

Sides 20 cm and 5 cm
(A rectangle is a special kind of parallelogram.)

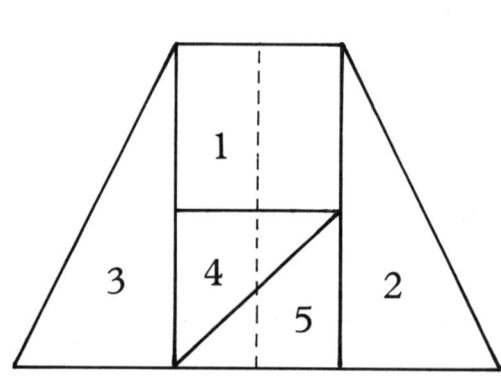

Sides 11 cm and 10 cm

d

Fourth side is 11 cm.

e

f

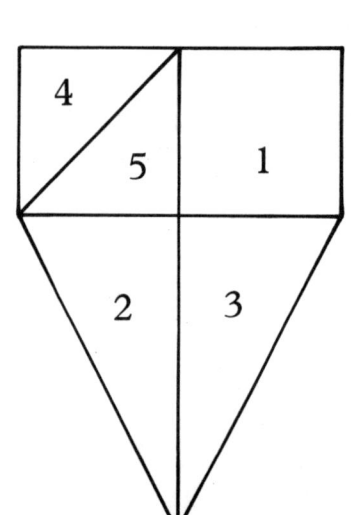

g

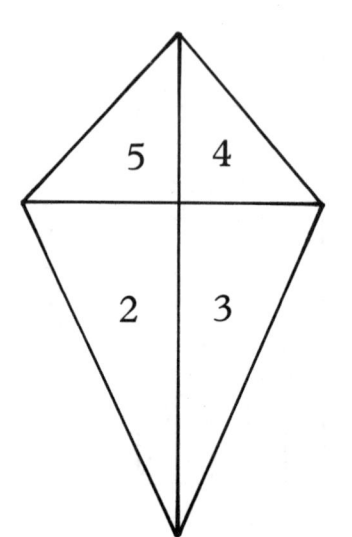

Tangram E consists of two squares, one oblong and four right-angled triangles, two of which are isosceles. Tangram F has one square and eight right-angled isosceles triangles, four large and four small.

Tangram E   Tangram F

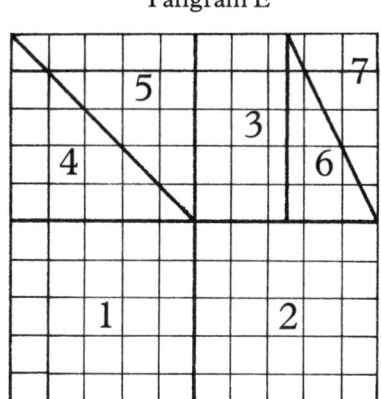 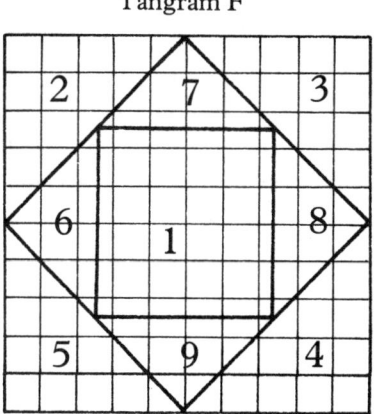

6 a

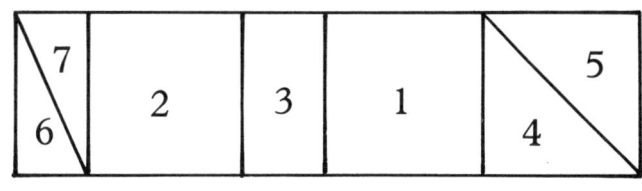

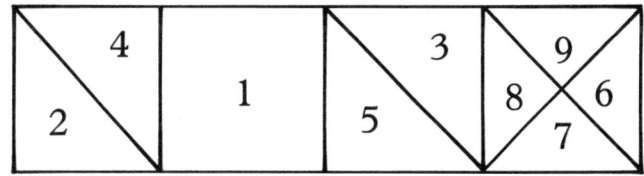

Length 20 cm   Width 5 cm   Perimeter 50 cm   Area 100 cm²

b

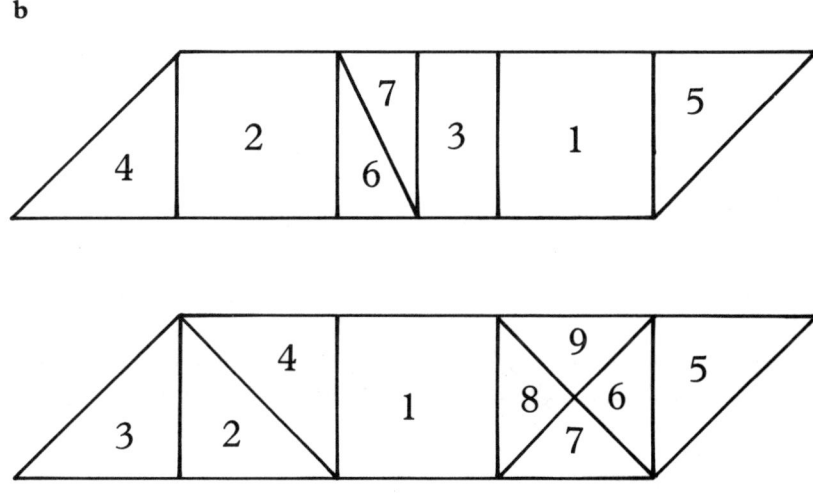

Sides 20 cm and 7 cm   Perimeter 54 cm   Area 100 cm²

c

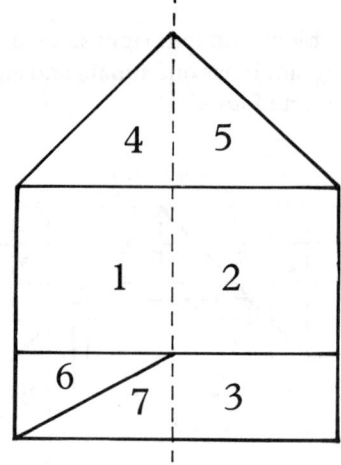

Pentagon with one axis of symmetry
Perimeter 39 cm. Area 100 cm²

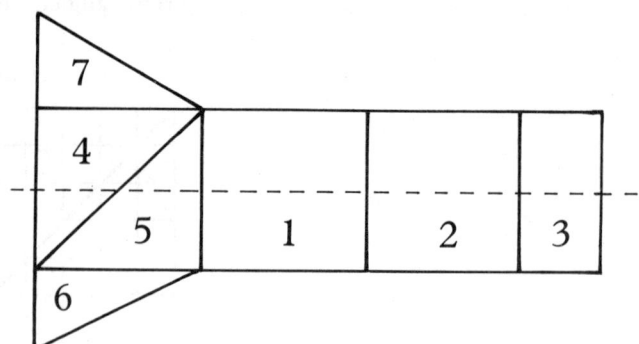

Hexagon with one axis of symmetry
Perimeter 51 cm.   Area 100 cm²

d

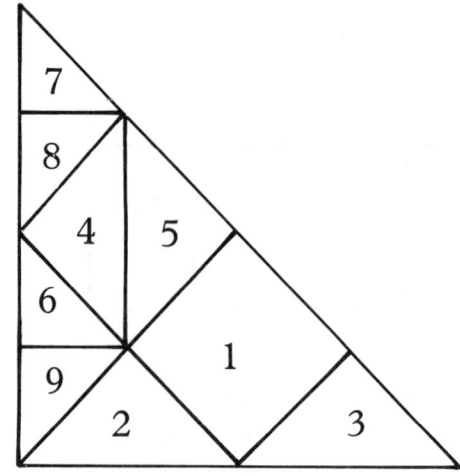

Two sides equal
Two angles equal

Perimeter 48 cm
Area 100 cm²

e

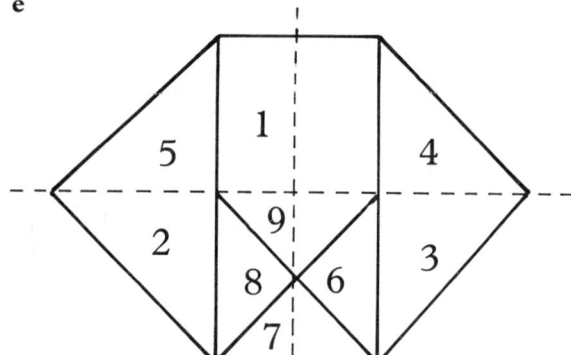

A regular hexagon has six axes of symmetry.

Tangram G

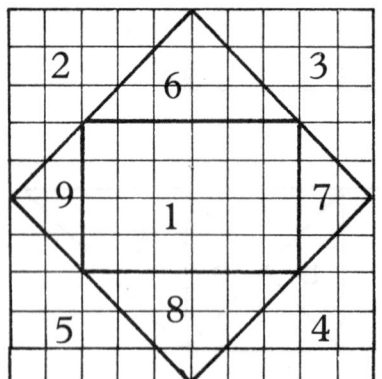

Tangram G is very similar to tangram F. The next question asks how they are the same and how they are different.

7 **a** Each tangram has four identical right-angled triangles (2, 3, 4, 5). In F the triangles 6, 7, 8 and 9 are identical. In G the triangles are of three different sizes: 6 and 8 are identical and the smaller triangles 7 and 9 are identical. F contains a square; G contains an oblong.
   b 20 cm   **c** 24 cm²   **d** 50 cm²   **e** 26 cm².

Skeleton solids

1 The construction of skeleton solids is an absorbing activity which can provide lasting satisfaction. Art or drink straws, cocktail sticks and angle card are readily available and easily manipulated. Wooden applicator sticks sold by chemists, or 'Craft Sticks' from E. J. Arnold, are about 15 cm long and so offer scope for cutting into different sizes and creating a wide variety of models. The ends need pointing to pierce polystyrene spheres but, alternatively, the ends may be carefully filed to the correct angle and joined by glue. The work is delicate and skilful hands are required to produce neat models.

Whichever material is used, the results are attractive and remarkably stable. They can be adapted for Christmas decorations if coloured straws and sticks are used or by lining angle-card models with tissue paper.

2 Of more mathematical interest is the fact that the number of vertices and edges can now be more clearly seen and counted than they can on closed solids.

Pupils should enter the number of vertices, edges and faces of any model they make, in the table.

An alternative activity is the construction of a shape from a given number of spheres and sticks.

| Name of solid | Number of | | |
	Faces	Vertices	Edges
Tetrahedron	4	4	6
Cube	6	8	12
Square pyramid	5	5	8
Octahedron	8	6	12
Hexahedron	6	5	9
Icosahedron	20	12	30

Some pupils may be able to spot the relationship between the number of faces, vertices and edges:

$$F + V = E + 2$$

which is associated with Leonard Euler (1707–1783), a gifted Swiss mathematician. However, the formula was known centuries earlier to Archimedes (287–212 BC).

Pupils frequently hear the names of great musicians, writers and artists of the past, yet the equally creative work of mathematicians remains largely unknown to them. Of them all, Archimedes is probably the greatest. Pre-eminent as a mathematician, he is also remembered for his many mechanical inventions.

Angle card demonstrates the same mechanical principle as angle iron: angling causes rigidity, as any fisherman frozen on a river bank will testify!

The effectiveness of angle card can be demonstrated by holding a flat strip of thin card between finger and thumb. Try to balance a coin on the other end of the card, choosing a coin which is just too heavy to be supported.

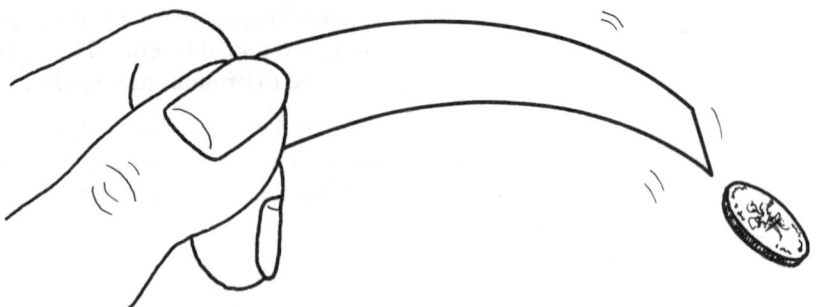

Now score the strip longitudinally and fold. Try again.

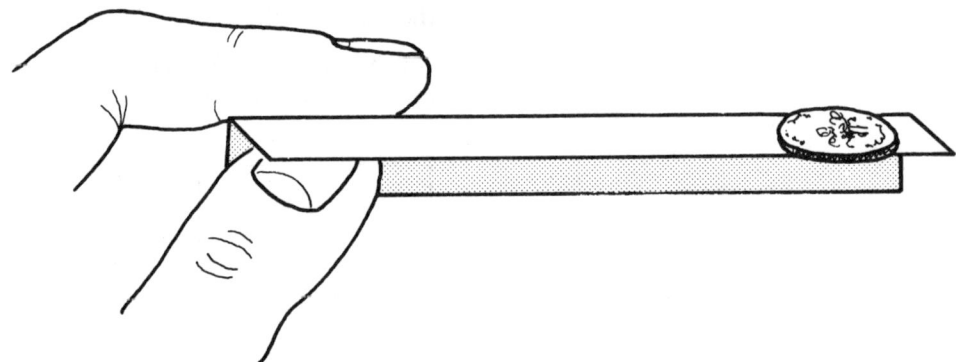

6 The octahedron made from twelve strips looks like this.

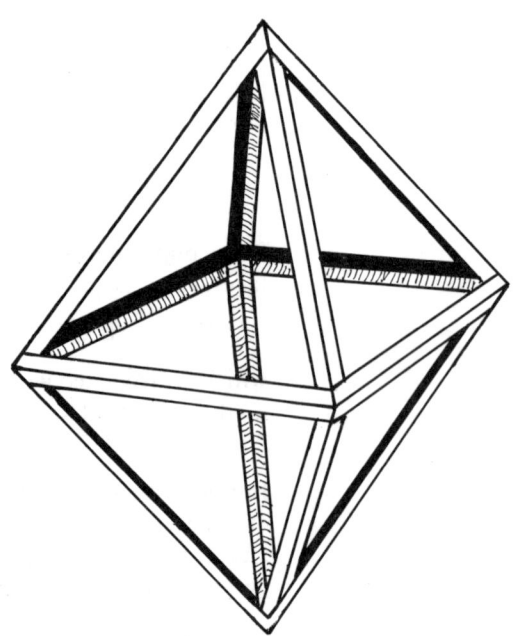

1 The idea of an exploded view was introduced earlier in this *Teachers' Book*; now it is the pupils' turn to become acquainted.

2 This is a reminder of the jigsaw property of the set of pentominoes; the diagram in the *Pupils' Book* shows only one of the many ways in which they can be fitted into a rectangle measuring 15 by 4 units. They will also fit into rectangles of 10 by 6, 12 by 5 and 20 by 3 units.

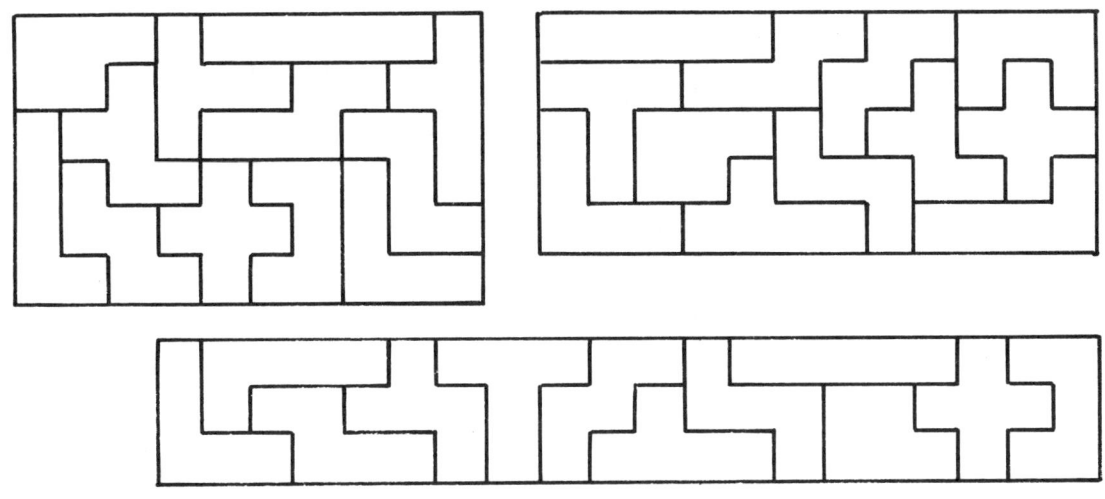

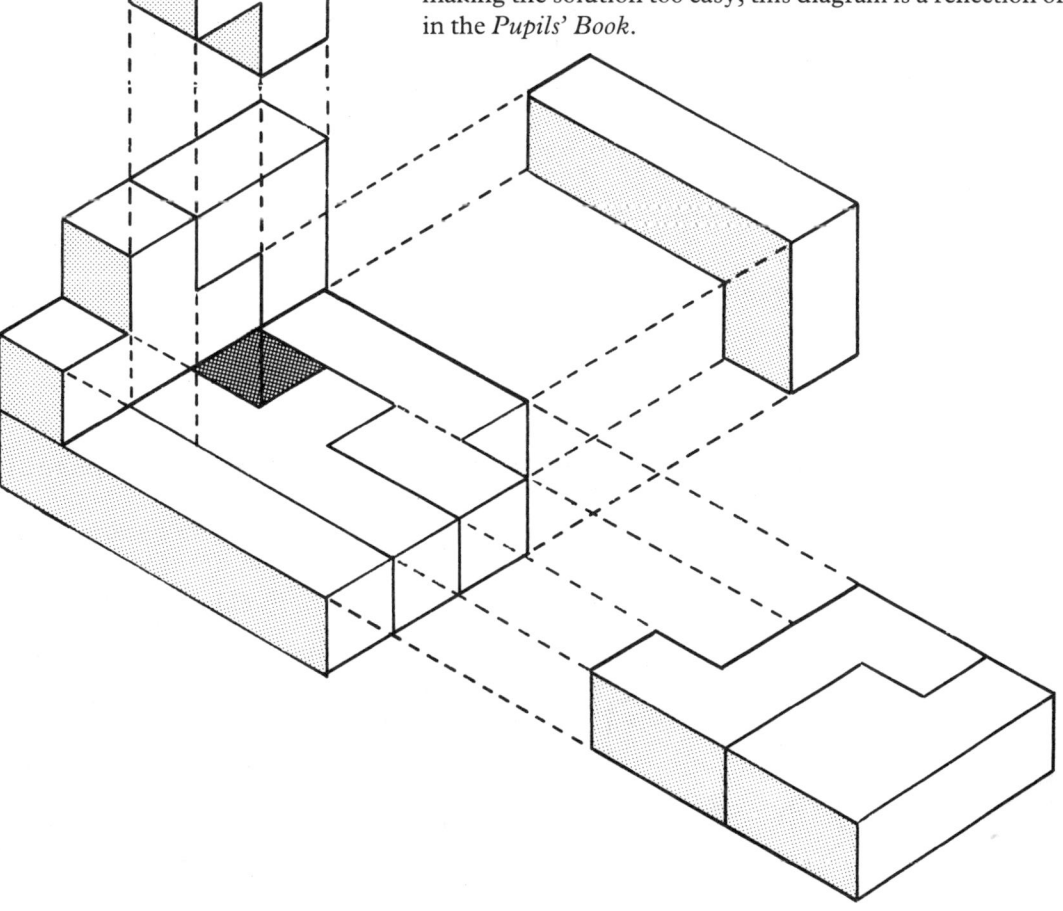

Similarly, the solid pentominoes can be used as three-dimensional jigsaw pieces to form cuboids. The diagram in the *Pupils' Book* gives just sufficient clues to help a pupil build a cuboid measuring $5 \times 4 \times 3$ and hence a volume of 60 cubic units. If a further clue is needed, perhaps this diagram could be shown to the pupils.

Nine solid pentominoes are shown in a partially exploded view. The remaining three complete the top layer in two different ways. To avoid making the solution too easy, this diagram is a reflection of the diagram in the *Pupils' Book*.

Another cuboid, measuring 6 × 5 × 2 units, can be made in two separate layers each 6 × 5.

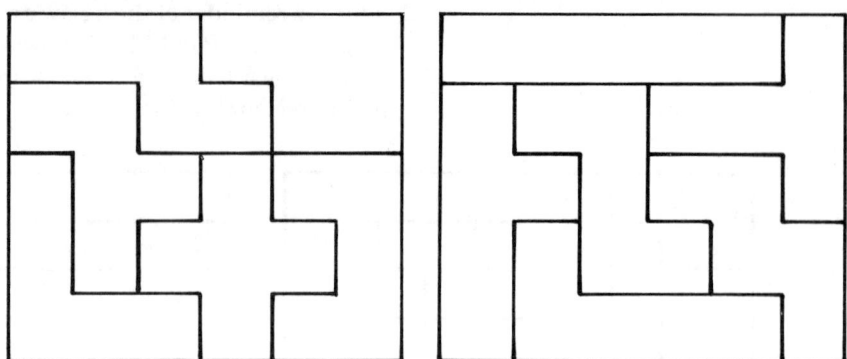

A cuboid measuring 2 × 3 × 10 is made in two layers but with three solid pentominoes fitted in upright positions to link the two layers together.

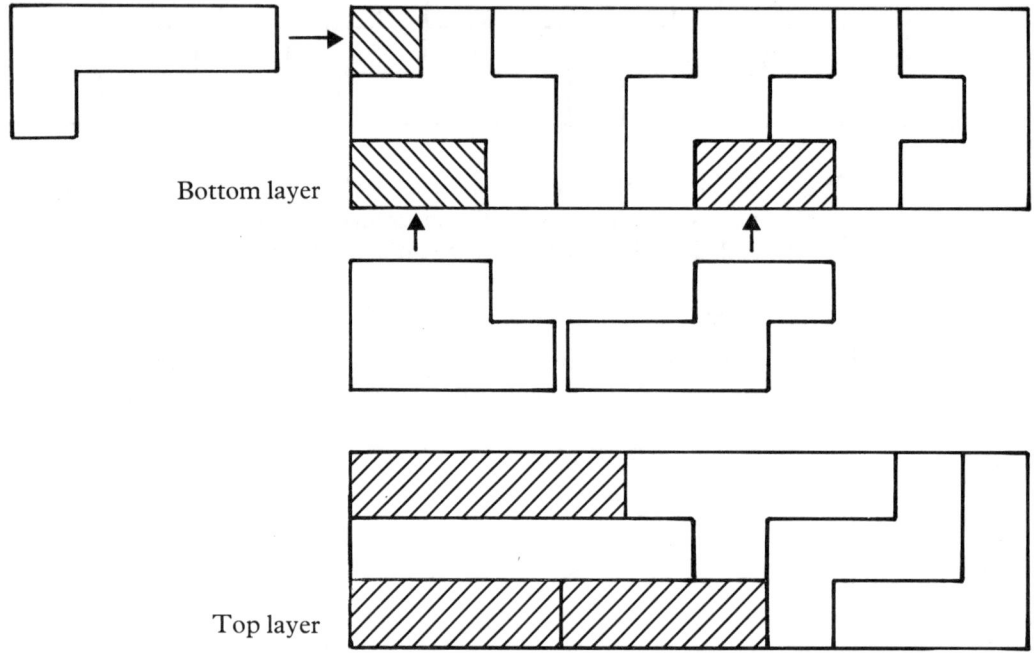

Bottom layer

Top layer

Drawing solid shapes 2   Pupils' Book page 21

3 Piet Hein, a Danish writer, experimented with an idea for a puzzle which
  involved fitting up to four cubes together in as many different ways as
  possible. He decided to ignore the five cuboid shapes pictured here:

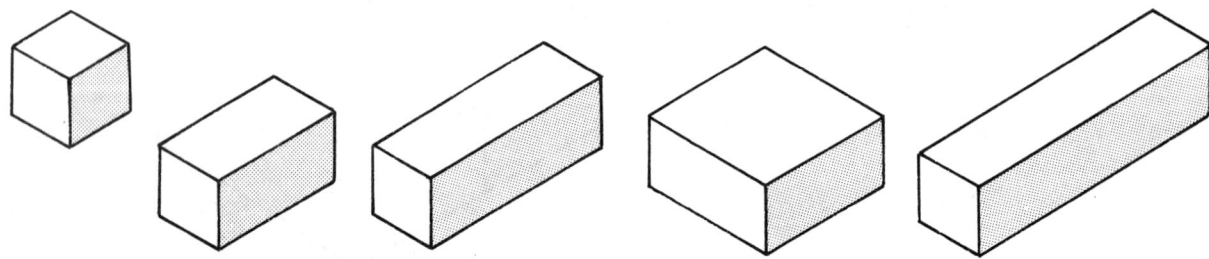

He was then left with seven irregular shapes: one made up from three cubes and six each made up from four cubes – a total of 27 cubes forming seven shapes. Now 27 is the cube of 3, and, surprise surprise, the seven pieces do fit together to make a 3 × 3 × 3 cube!

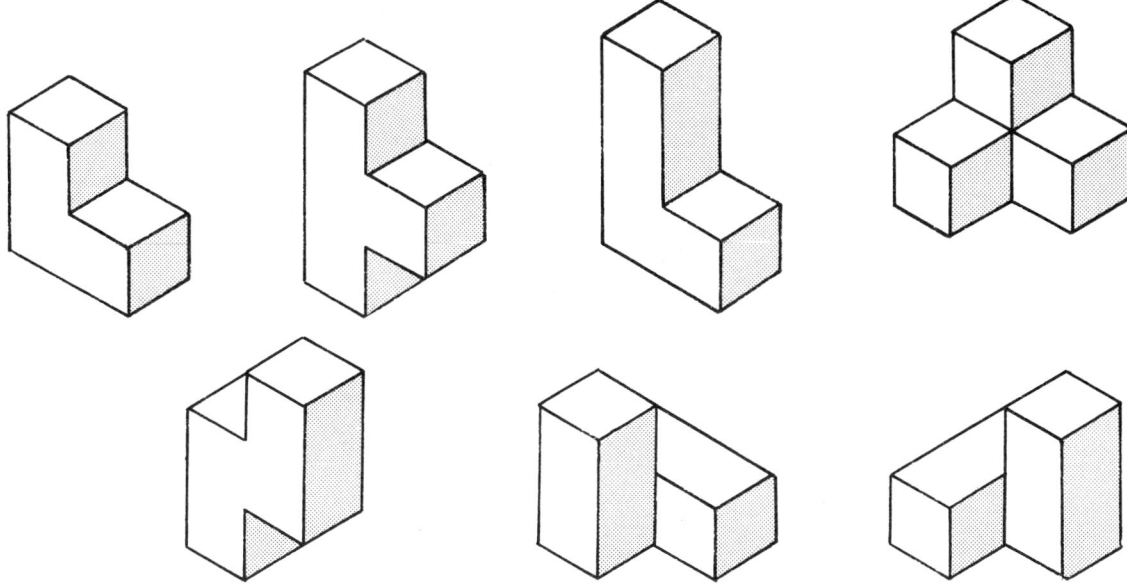

Notice that the last two shapes appear to be the same, but one is the reflection of the other so that you have a pair – one 'left-handed' and the other 'right-handed'.

4 The completion of the blanks in the two tabulations reveals the beginnings of the multiplication square. The sequence from 1 × 1 to 4 × 4 is shown below with the total number of cubes used for each 'skyscraper'. (Most commercial sets of cubes provide base plates as an extra and these are helpful in giving stability to the skyscraper.)

The link in this activity between terms in the series of square numbers and the series of triangular numbers is a further interesting example of the interplay between the various figurate numbers. Pupils will have encountered previous examples in *Challengers B*.

									4	8	12	16
					3	6	9		3	6	9	12
		2	4		2	4	6		2	4	6	8
1		1	2		1	2	3		1	2	3	4

      1   9   36   100 . . . .

In each case the total number of cubes used to build the skyscraper is a square number, though not every square number is used. The sequence is worth investigating by the pupils to see how many square numbers are omitted between successive terms.

When the square roots are written below each square number, they form the terms of the series of triangular numbers.

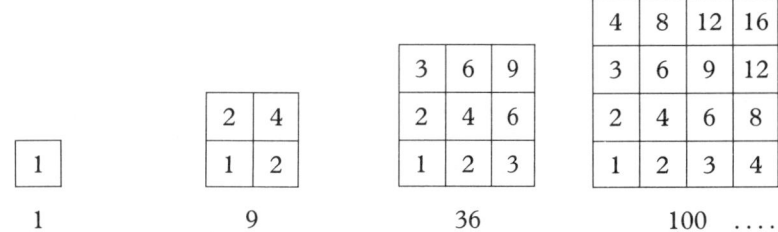

     1   3   6   10 . . . .

The next term (multiplication tables 1–5) will be 15, the square root of 225, and then (tables 1–6) will be 21, the square root of 441, and so on.

Polyshapes 2

The work on 'Polyshapes' can be extended by using a shape other than a square as the basic unit. Area conservation, symmetry, rotation and reflection can all be reinforced in interesting ways by the study of *polyiamonds*. In the first instance the polyiamonds are generated from equilateral triangles and recording is done on isometric grid paper.

1 No. The *diamond* and *triamond* shown in the *Pupils' Book* are the only ones possible.

2 The other two *tetriamonds* are:

3 The other three *pentiamonds* are:

4 Children should be encouraged to find the twelve possible *hexiamonds* shown in the table below by taking each pentiamond in turn and adding a moniamond to it in a systematic way, eliminating duplicates as they go

5 a Only two of the twelve hexiamonds are even:

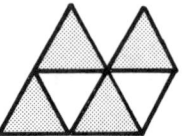 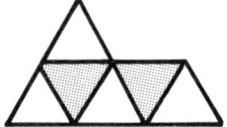

b The hexiamond in the shape of regular hexagon has a perimeter of six units.

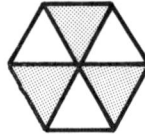

Polyshapes 2

6

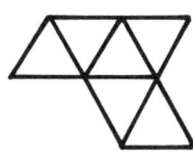

Pistol

Hexagon

Hockey stick

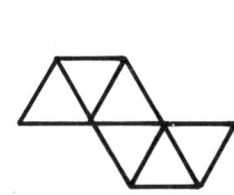

Snake

Arrow

Butterfly

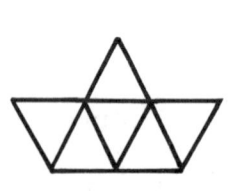

Crown

Hook

Parallelogram

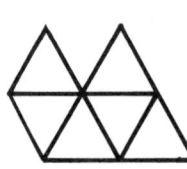

Yacht

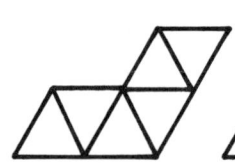

Chevron

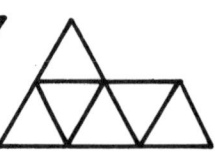

Sphinx

7 Every hexiamond tessellates on its own – here are some examples:

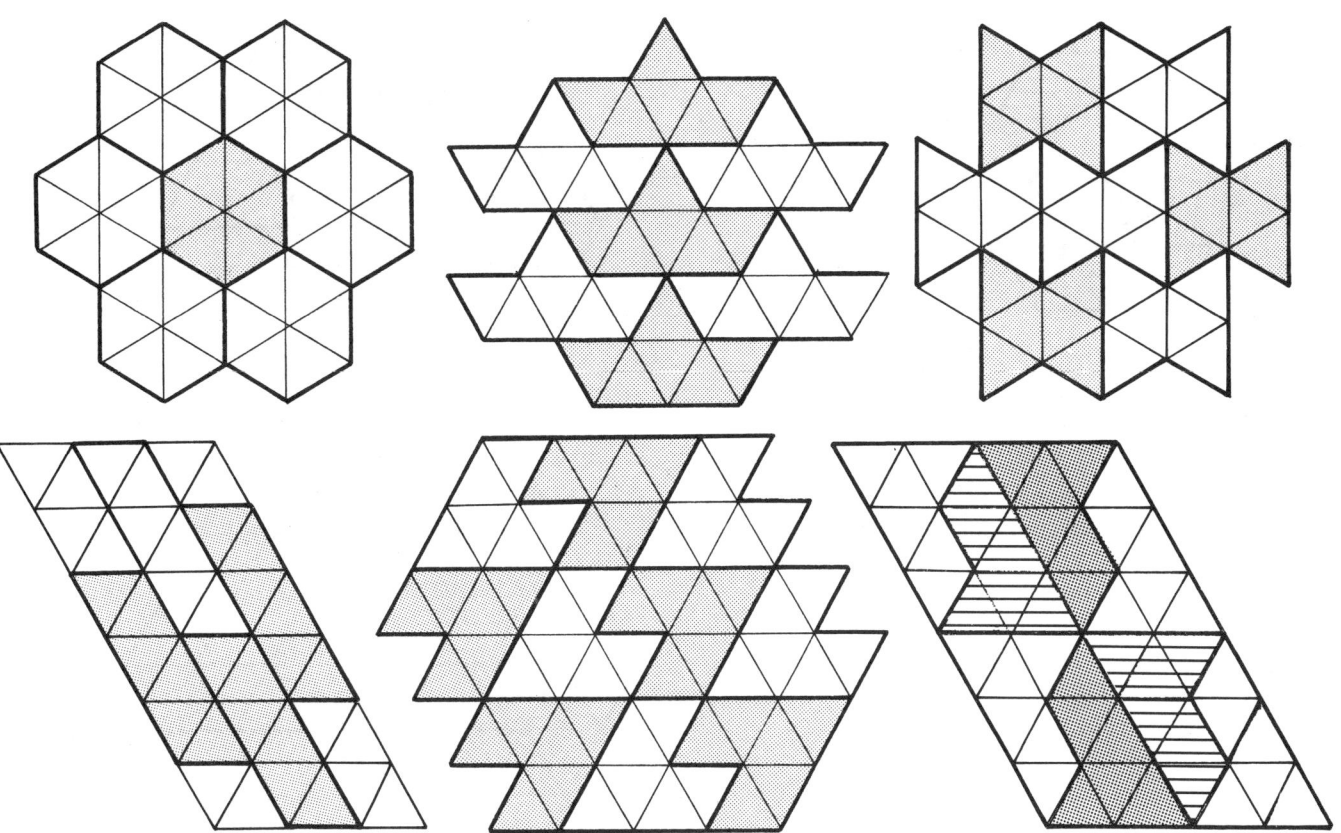

8 Here are some, but not all, of the possible examples of parallelograms made from hexiamonds:

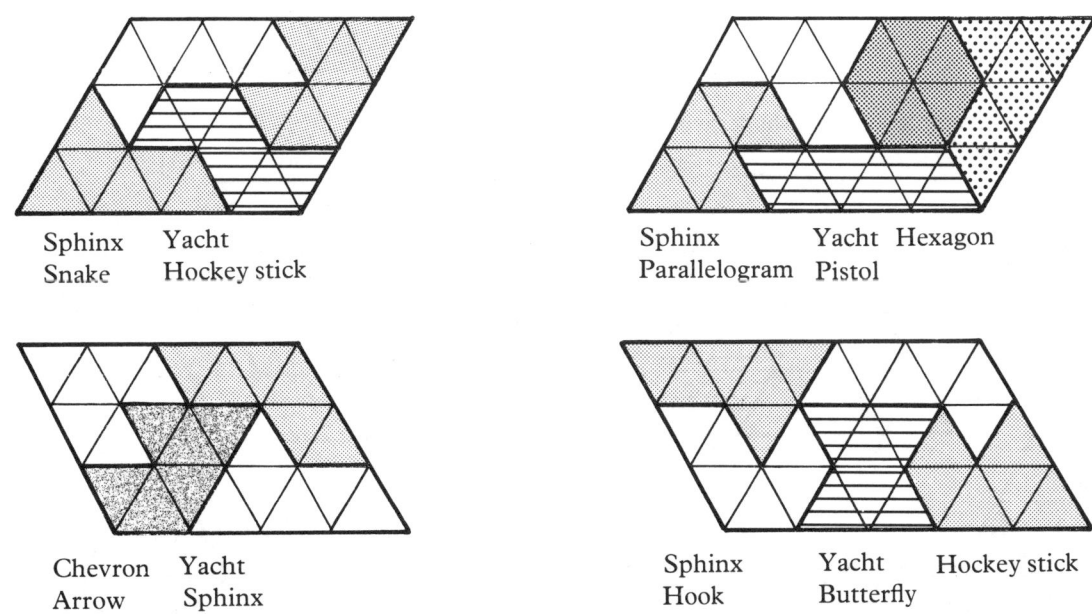

Sphinx   Yacht
Snake   Hockey stick

Sphinx   Yacht   Hexagon
Parallelogram   Pistol

Chevron   Yacht
Arrow   Sphinx

Sphinx   Yacht   Hockey stick
Hook   Butterfly

If using the same hexiamond more than once is allowed, there are even more possibilities. For example:

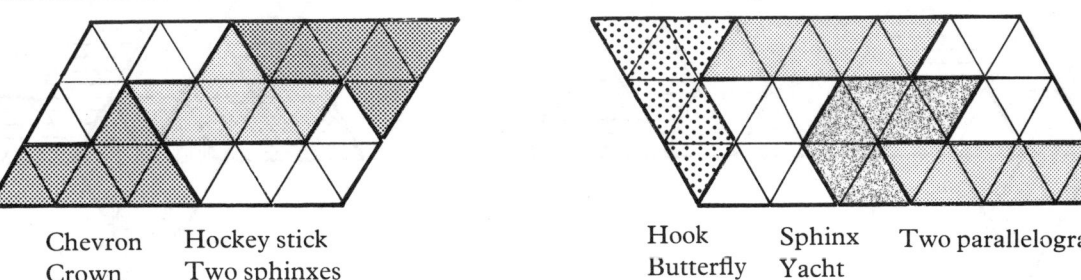

Chevron   Hockey stick
Crown   Two sphinxes

Hook   Sphinx   Two parallelograms
Butterfly Yacht

9 Some examples of regular hexagons which can be made without duplicating hexiamonds are:

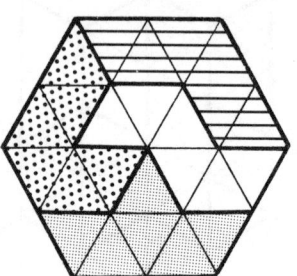

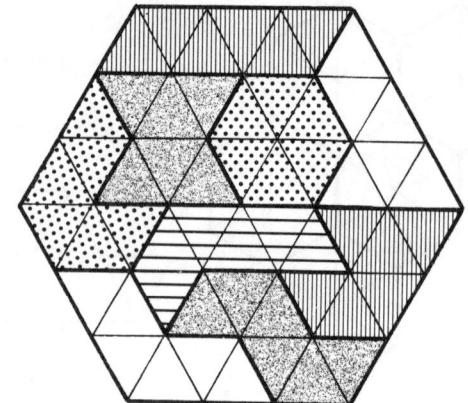

Chevron, Hook
Snake, Crown

Parallelogram
Butterfly
Chevron
Yacht
Snake
Sphinx
Hexagon
Hook
Hockey stick

If duplicate hexiamonds are allowed, this
regular hexagon can be made from sixteen pieces:

Parallelogram, Butterfly, Hook,
Chevron, Yacht, Crown,
Two hexagons, Two hockey sticks,
Three arrows, Three sphinxes

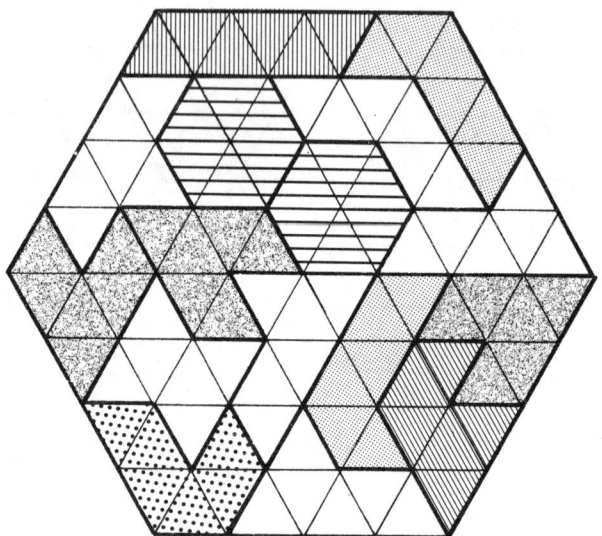

Here are some examples of other shapes which can be made:

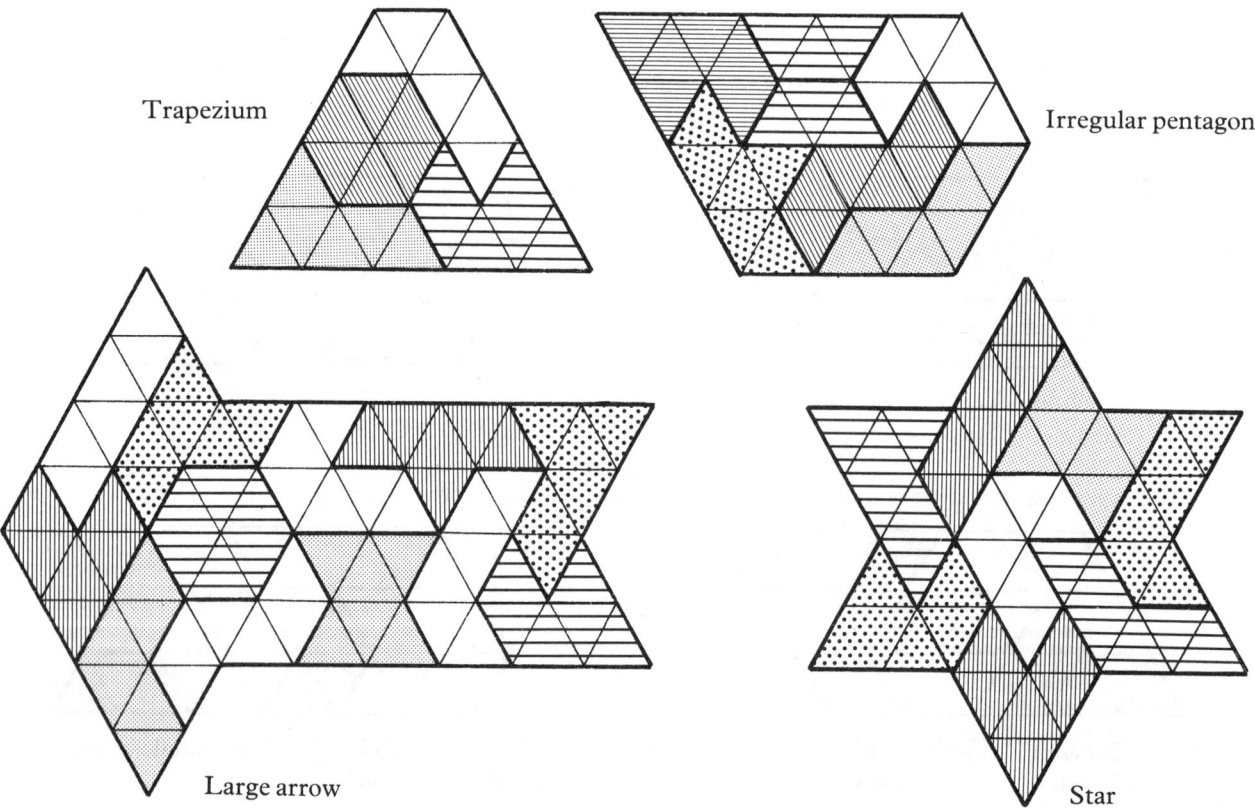

Trapezium

Irregular pentagon

Large arrow

Star

If instead of the equilateral triangle, a right-angled scalene triangle is chosen as the motif, similar investigations can be carried out.

The new shapes could be called *right polyiamonds*, but pupils might well invent their own name.

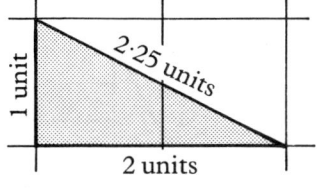

The triangles should be drawn and cut out from squared paper. As each triangle has an area of 1 square unit, the areas of shapes generated will be easy to calculate or count. The hypotenuse of each triangle is $\sqrt{5}$ which could be 'rounded up' to 2·25 or $2\frac{1}{4}$ units so that approximate perimeters can be found.

10

Rectangle	f
Isosceles triangle	a,b
Parallelogram	e,c
Kite	d

Shape	Area (square units)	Perimeter (units)
a	2	6·5
b	2	8·5
c	2	8·5
d	2	6·0
e	2	6·0
f	2	6·0

11 These are some of the ways in which one triangle can be added to make a new shape. Each *right triamond* has an area of 3 square units. Grouping right triamonds according to their perimeter lengths makes it easier to check for duplicates. They could also be sorted into those which are symmetrical and those which are not.

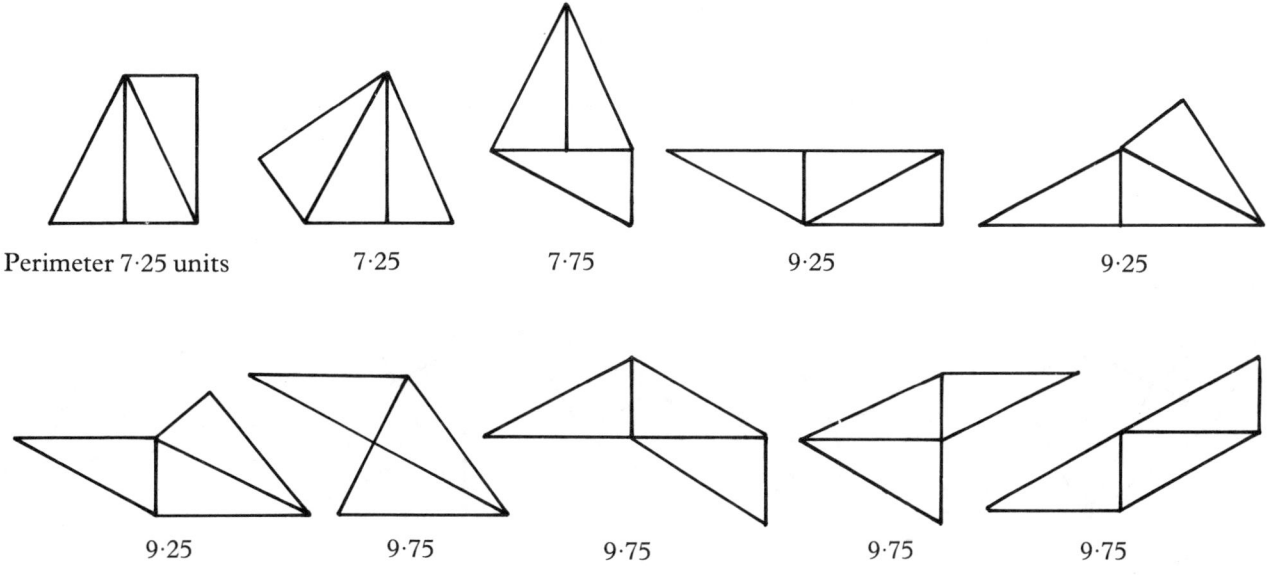

Perimeter 7·25 units   7·25   7·75   9·25   9·25

        9·25   9·75   9·75   9·75   9·75

12 Here are some possibilities for shapes made from four right-angled scalene triangles – *right tetriamonds* – all of which have an area of 4 square units. Again, grouping by perimeter lengths makes it easier to find duplicates.

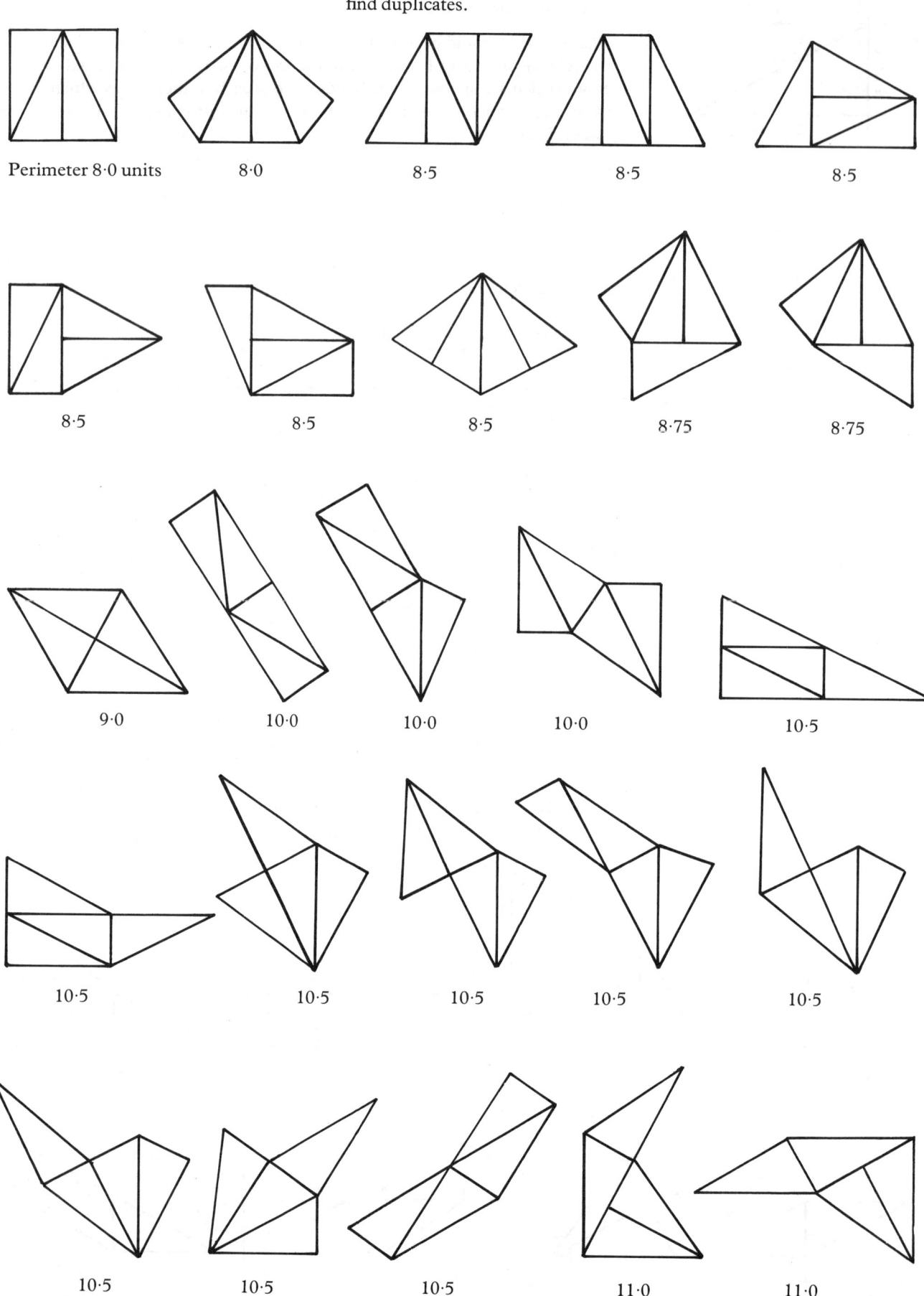

Perimeter 8·0 units   8·0   8·5   8·5   8·5

8·5   8·5   8·5   8·75   8·75

9·0   10·0   10·0   10·0   10·5

10·5   10·5   10·5   10·5   10·5

10·5   10·5   10·5   11·0   11·0

Polyshapes 2 — Pupils' Book page 24 continued

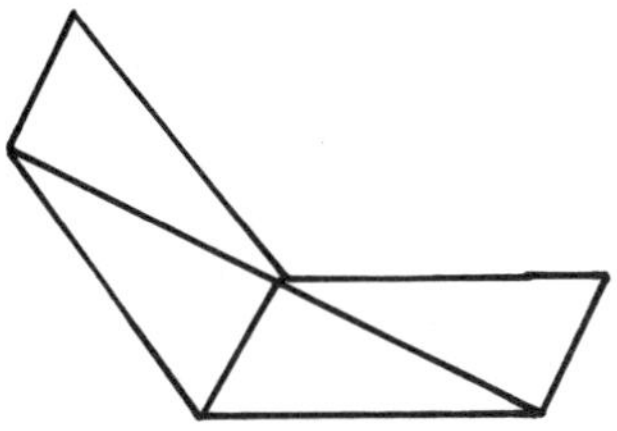

11·0

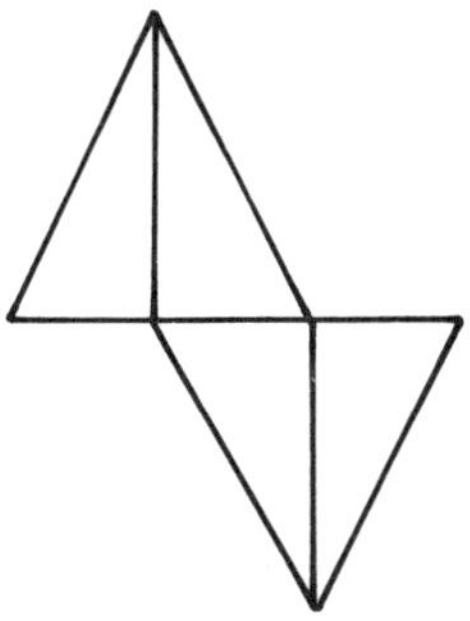

11·0

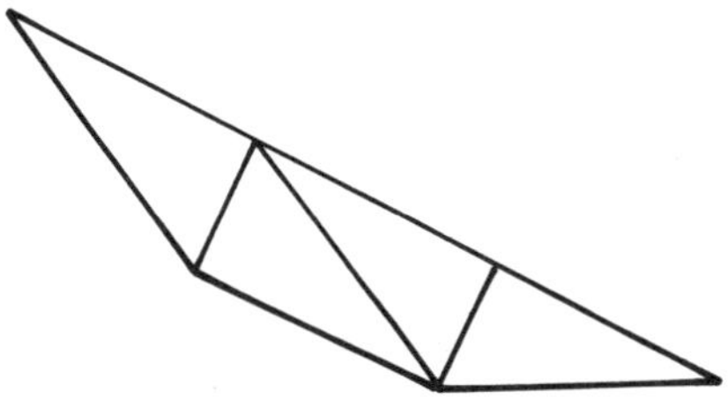

12·5

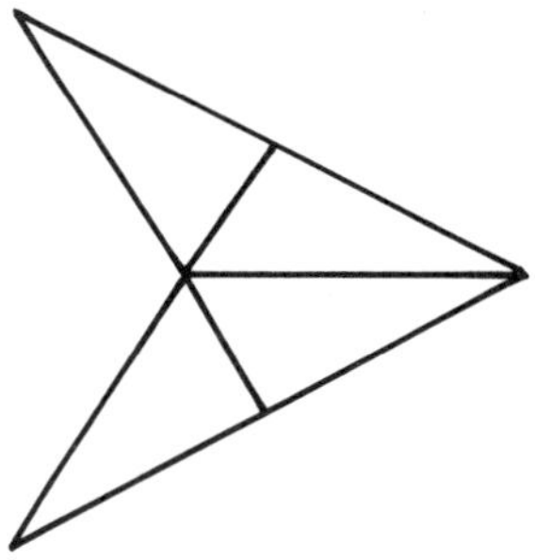

12·5

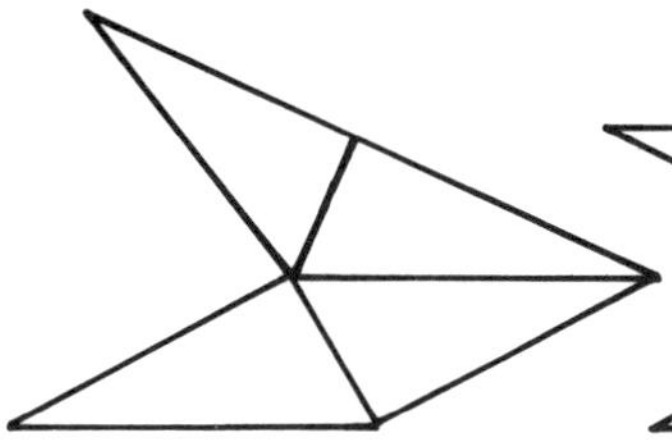

12·5

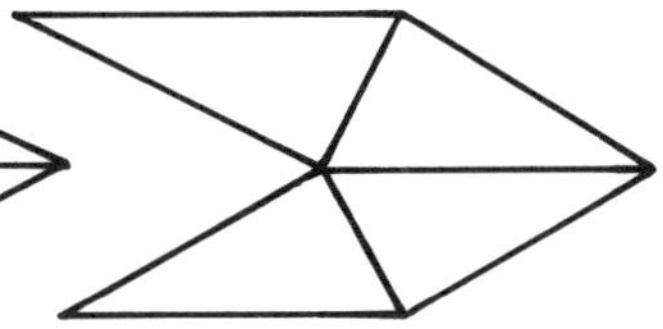

12·5

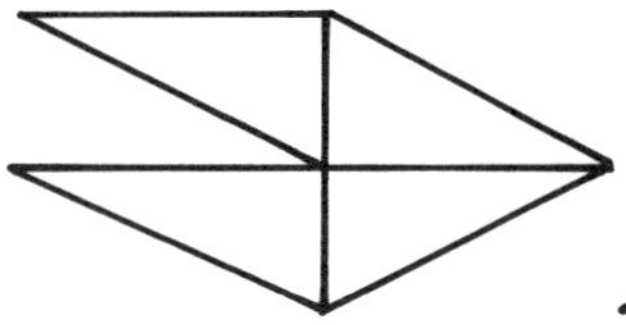

13·0

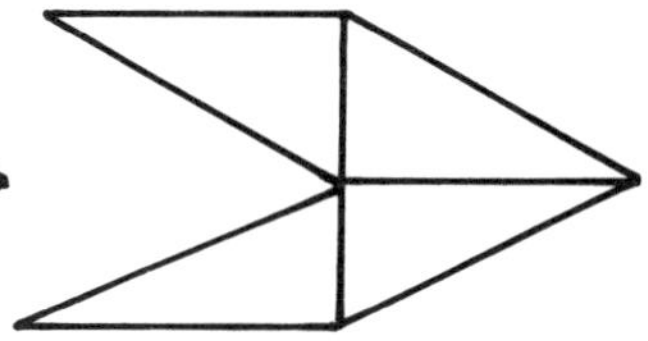

13·0

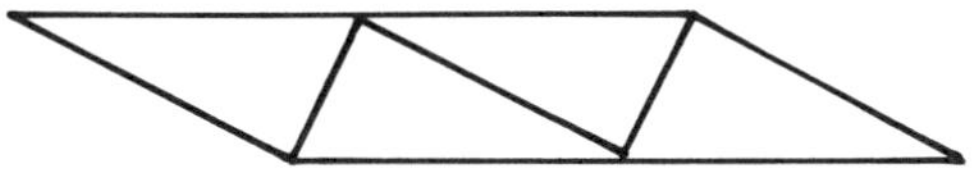

13·0

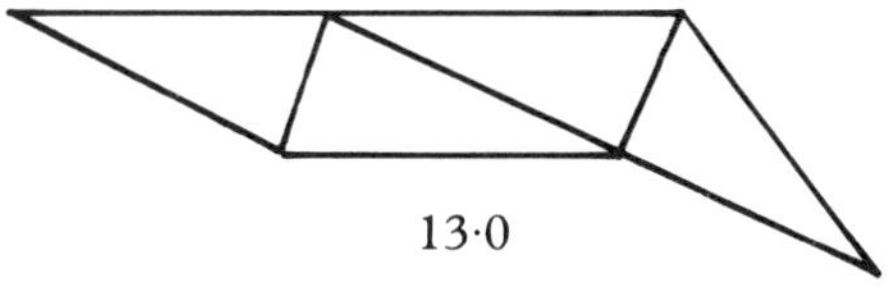

13·0

As an alternative, *right polyiamonds* could be generated using a 3:4:5 right-angled triangle as a motif. The area of each triangle is then 6 square units and all the perimeters would be a whole number of units. Some of the polyiamonds listed in questions **11** and **12** could not be made, as it will no longer be possible to join two single-unit sides to a two-unit side.

One way to check the perimeter of a right polyiamond is to multiply the perimeter of one triangle by the number of triangles used and then subtract *twice* the lengths of the touching sides.

In the example, four triangles, each with a perimeter of 5·25 units, are used to generate a right tetriamond. The touching sides $(2+2+2{\cdot}25)$ add up to 6·25 units, so the perimeter is given by:

$$p = 4(5{\cdot}25) - 2(6{\cdot}25) = 21 - 12{\cdot}5 = 8{\cdot}5 \text{ units}$$

Polyshapes 2 — Pupils' Book page 25

Polytraps (Polytrapezia)

This time the motif is an *isosceles trapezium* with an area of 2 square units and an approximate perimeter of 6·8 units.

By joining sides of the same length, *polytraps* are generated and given names such as *dotraps, trotraps, tetrotraps*, etc.

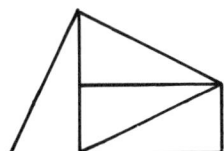

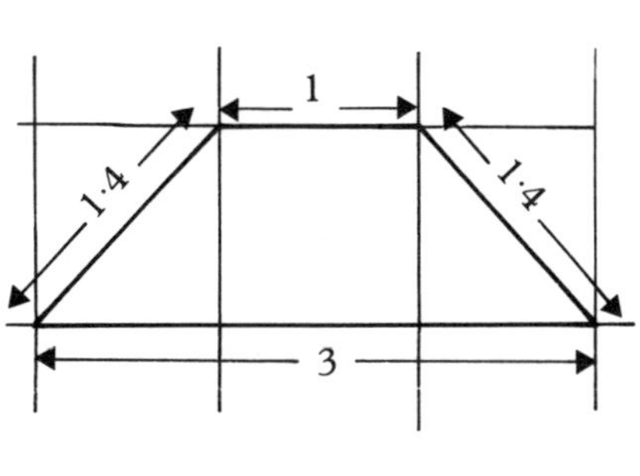

13 and 14 Dotraps, each with an area of 4 square units. Axes of symmetry are marked.

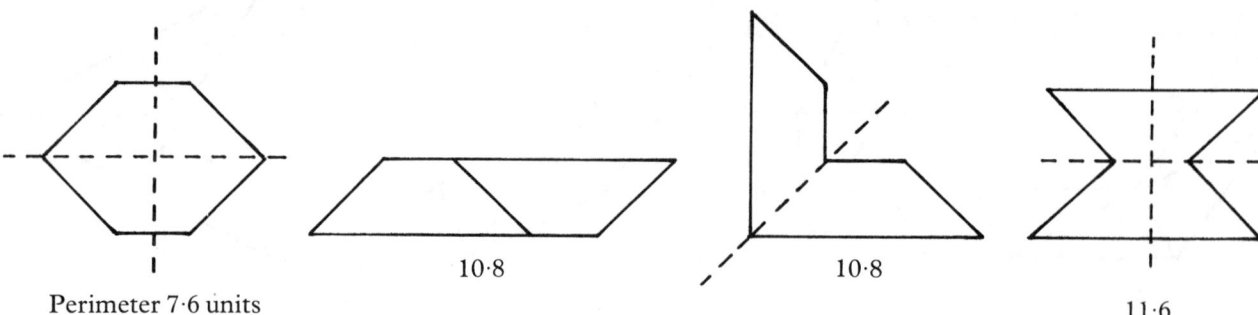

Perimeter 7·6 units   10·8   10·8   11·6

Trotraps, each with an area of 6 square units. Axes of symmetry are marked.

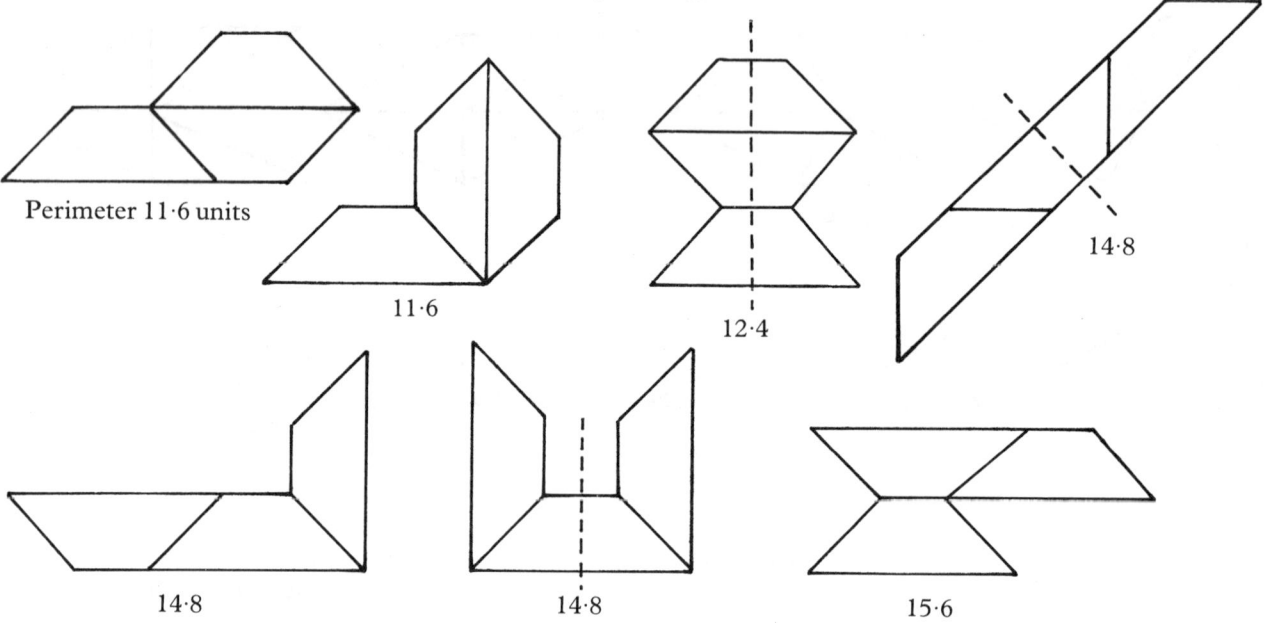

Perimeter 11·6 units   11·6   12·4   14·8

14·8   14·8   15·6

Tetrotraps, each with an area of 8 square units. Axes of symmetry are marked.

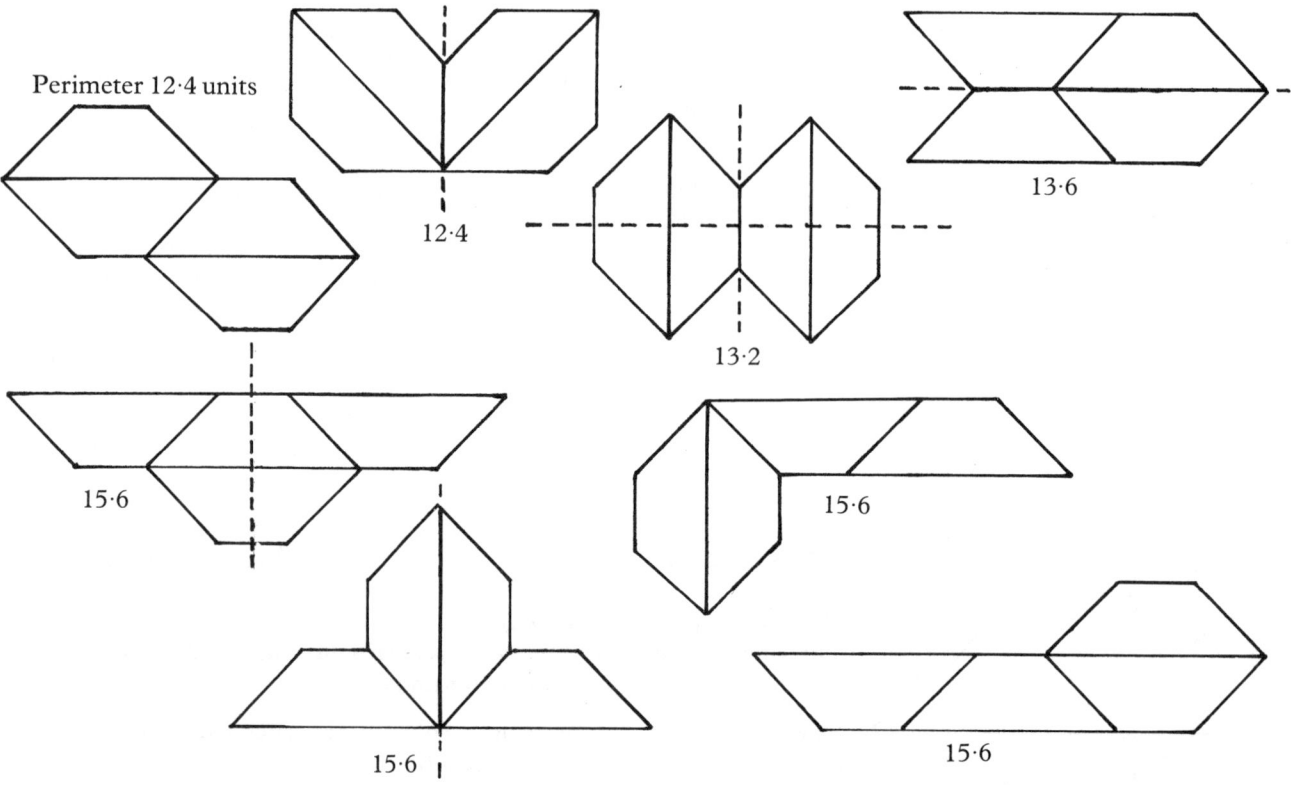

Perimeter 12·4 units   12·4   13·2   13·6

15·6   15·6   15·6   15·6

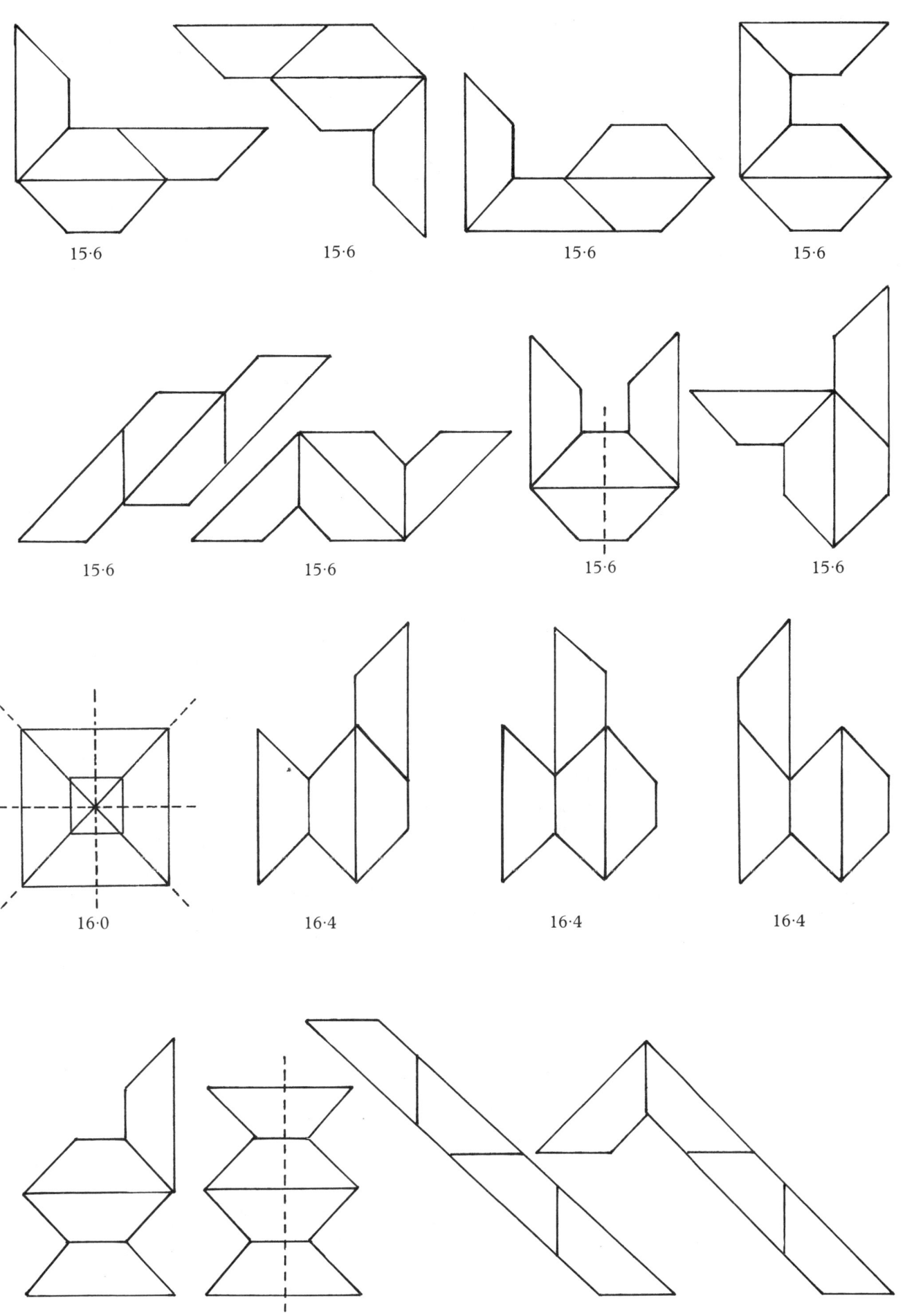

15·6   15·6   15·6   15·6

15·6   15·6   15·6   15·6

16·0   16·4   16·4   16·4

16·4   17·2   18·8   18·8

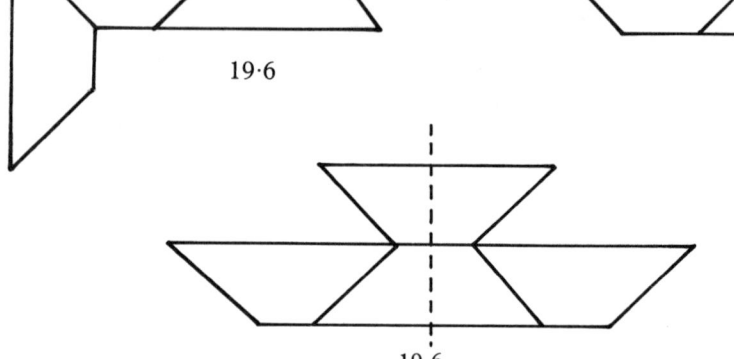

18·8   18·8   18·8   19·6

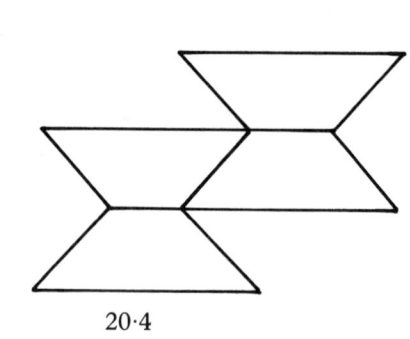

19·6   19·6

19·6

20·4

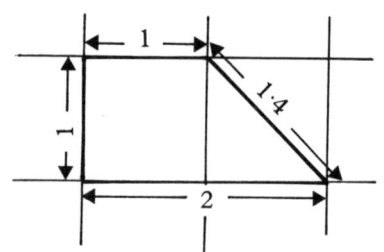

15 Tessellation investigation.

16 a Area 8 square units, perimeter 13·6 units.
  b Area 10 square units, perimeter 20·4 units.
  c Area 12 square units, perimeter 21·2 units.

As an additional alternative, some pupils may wish to investigate *right polytraps* which are based on a right-angled trapezium with an area of $1\frac{1}{2}$ square units and an approximate perimeter of 5·4 units.

The work in 'Pinboard Activities' is extended to investigate the classification of shapes by the number of pins on the boundary and the number of pins enclosed by the boundary. This idea is extended further to the 4 by 4 or 16-pin board.

1 a 2 square units

b

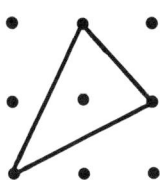

$1\frac{1}{2}$ square units

c When there is one pin inside the shape, the number of square units in the area is equal to half the number of pins touched on the boundary.

2 These are some shapes with one pin untouched inside the boundary:

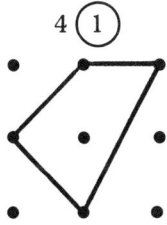   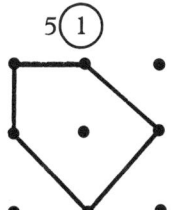   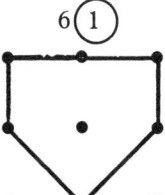   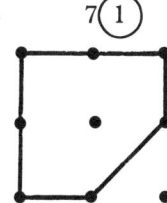

2 square units $2\frac{1}{2}$ square units   3 square units $3\frac{1}{2}$ square units

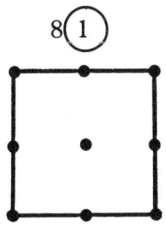

4 square units

3 a Square 4 ① 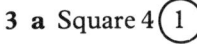   **b** Parallelogram 4 ①   **c** Kite 4 ①   **d** Trapezium 4 ①

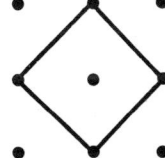   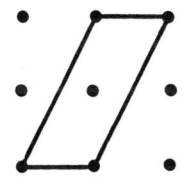   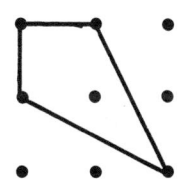   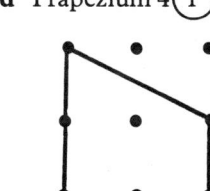

2 square units   2 square units   2 square units   3 square units

f   5·6 units   6·4 units   6·4 units   7·2 units

Shape	Name and classification	Area in square units	Perimeter in units	Axes of symmetry
	irregular quadrilateral 5 ①	$2\frac{1}{2}$	6·6	0
	square 8 ①	4	8	4
	irregular pentagon 5 ①	$2\frac{1}{2}$	6·2	1
	isosceles triangle 3 ①	$1\frac{1}{2}$	5·8	1
	irregular pentagon 7 ①	$3\frac{1}{2}$	7·4	1
	trapezium 6 ①	3	7·2	0

Pinboard Activities 2

Pupils' Book page 28

5 Z $5\frac{1}{2}$ W 5   U $4\frac{1}{2}$ V 4   X $3\frac{1}{2}$ Y 3 square units

7 U 10·2   Z 10   X 9·4   Y 9·2   W 8·8   V 8·4 units

8

a	4	④	4	4	8·8	4
b	6	②	5	4	8·8	0
c	7	③	6	$5\frac{1}{2}$	10	0
d	10	④	6	8	10·8	2
e	8	②	4	5	9·2	0
f	10	②	8	6	12·4	1

9 a

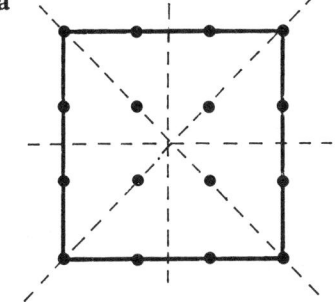

b

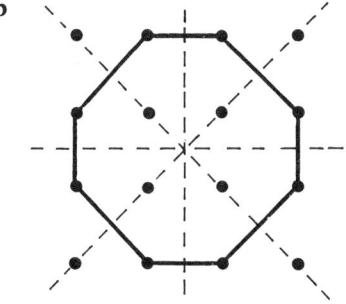

c

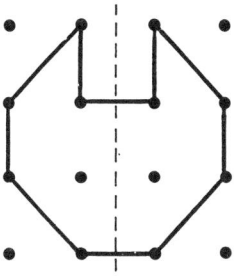

d

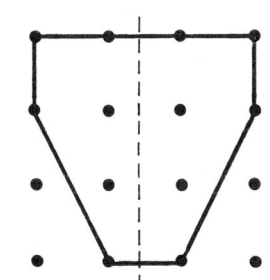

e

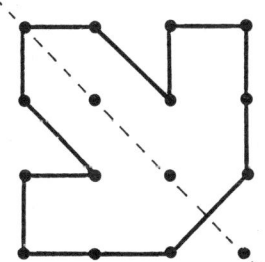

f

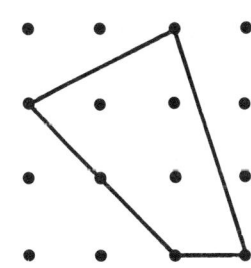

At this stage, *some* children may wish to investigate the relationship between the area of a polygon whose vertices lie on lattice points (in our case pins), the number of points (pins) on the boundary and the number of points (pins) inside the boundary. 'Pick's Theorem' gives a simple formula for this relationship:

$$A = \tfrac{1}{2}B + C - 1$$

Where A is the area, B is the number of pins on the boundary and C is the number of pins contained inside and untouched by the boundary.

Some examples:

In question **3d**, B = 6 and C = 1; so A = $\frac{1}{2}$(6) + 1 − 1 = 3 square units.
In question **8b**, B = 6 and C = 2; so A = $\frac{1}{2}$(6) + 2 − 1 = 4 square units.
In question **8c**, B = 7 and C = 3; so A = $\frac{1}{2}$(7) + 3 − 1 = $5\frac{1}{2}$ square units.
In question **9d**, B = 8 and C = 4; so A = $\frac{1}{2}$(8) + 4 − 1 = 7 square units.
In question **9f**, B = 5 and C = 3; so A = $\frac{1}{2}$(5) + 3 − 1 = $4\frac{1}{2}$ square units.

More Tangrams 2

Tangrams H and K are both developed from tangram C in 'More Tangrams 1'. They are all designed from a basic construction of 'joining each corner of the square in turn to the mid-point of the first opposite side, moving clockwise'. Before cutting out the tangrams, pupils should be reminded to mark the backs of the pieces with the correct letter.

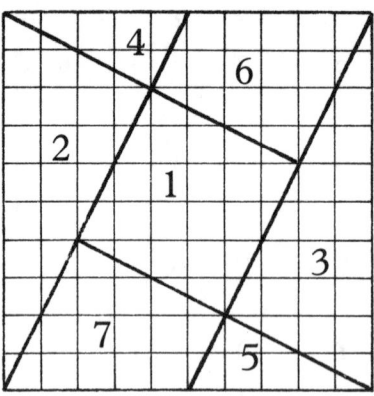 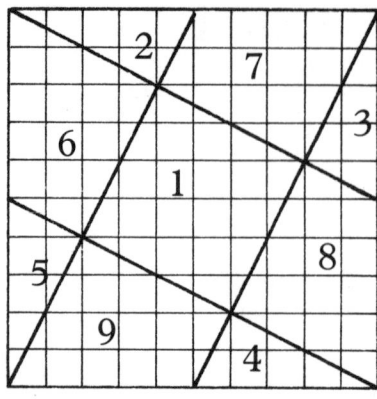

Tangram H   Tangram K

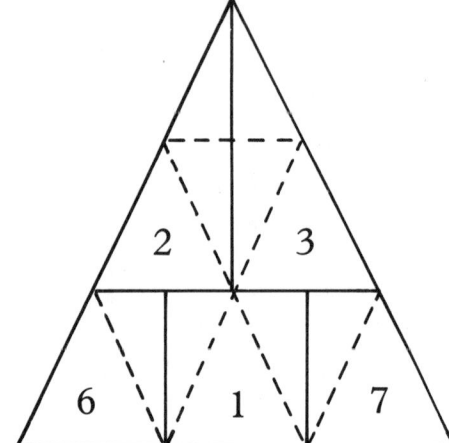

1 a The new shape is a *trapezium* – a quadrilateral with two sides parallel.

b Yes. No measurements are required; check by placing the pieces one on top of the other.

c After the two triangles have been formed, carefully place the small one on top of the large one and mark along the edges to show that the large triangle is nine times the area of the small triangle.

d A regular octagon has eight axes of symmetry.

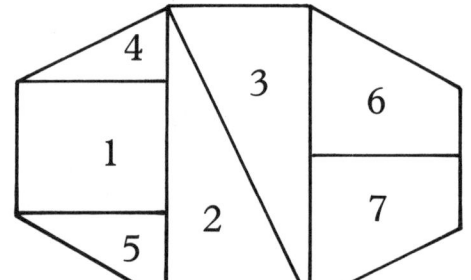

2 a

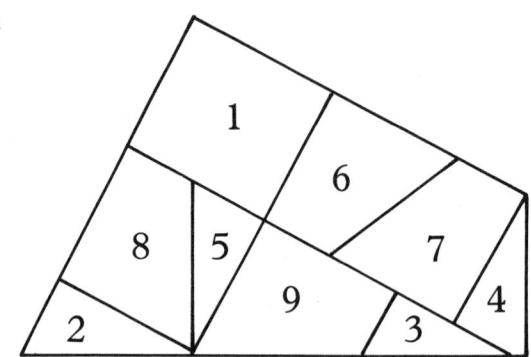

b Estimate.
c Approximate perimeter is 42 cm.

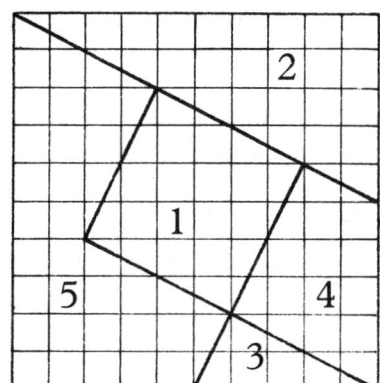

Tangram L

2 **d** The rectangle can be made by fitting two identical trapezia together. The length of the rectangle is the sum of the two parallel sides; its width is the perpendicular distance between them.

The area of each trapezium is half that of the rectangle; that is, *half the sum of the parallel sides multiplied by the perpendicular distance between them.*

3 Tangram L is based on the same construction as tangrams C, H and K. There are only five pieces, but the inclusion of a re-entrant hexagon leads to interesting possibilities.

Shape	Name of shape	Perimeter in centimetres		Area in square centimetres	
		estimate	measure	estimate	measure
	rectangle		40		100
	parallelogram		42		100
	right-angled scalene triangle		52		100
	St. George's Cross (or re-entrant dodecagon)		54		100
	irregular quadrilateral		$42\frac{1}{2}$		100

41

4 a The two right-angled triangles:

b The smaller triangle is a quarter of the area of the larger one. This can be shown, as in question **1c** by placing the smaller triangle on the larger.

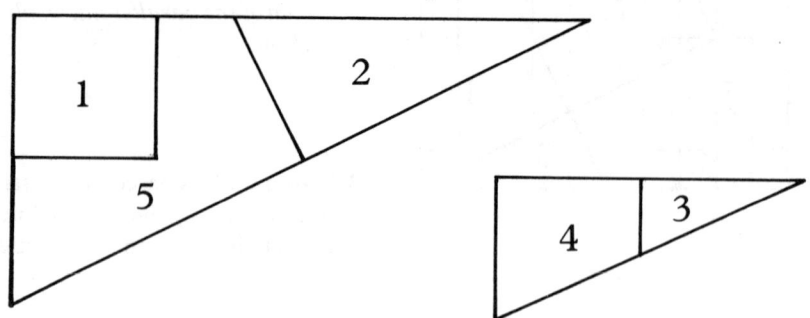

c and d Here are some letters which can be made – the St. George's Cross from question **3** could also be used as an 'X'. The children could investigate other possibilities.

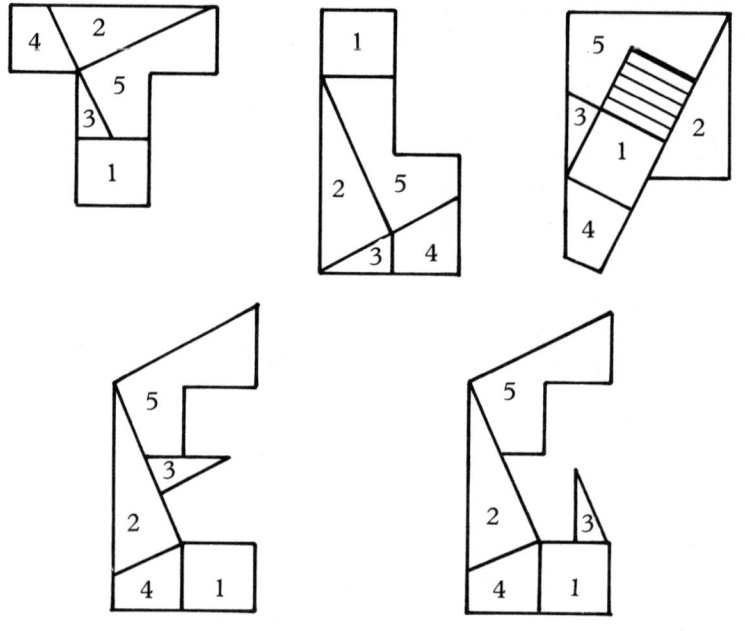

5 Tangram M consists of one rectangle, twice as long as it is wide, and four right-angled isosceles triangles.

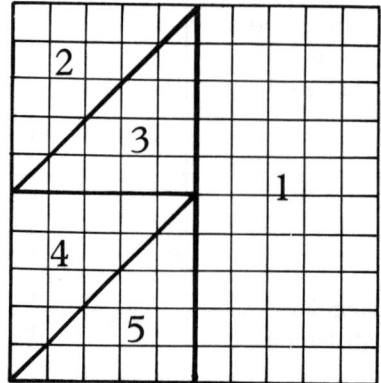

Tangram M

a The square and the triangle each have an area of 25 cm².

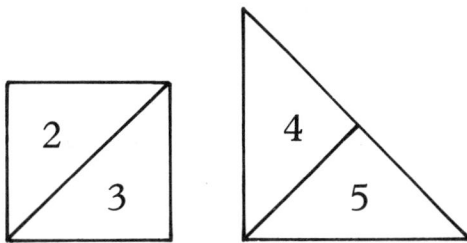

b The square has a perimeter of 20 cm, the triangle approximately 24 cm.

c The triangle has the greater perimeter by 4 cm.

d Yes

e

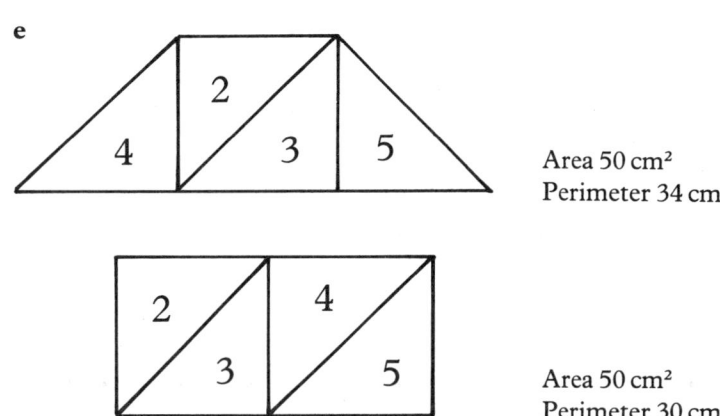

Area 50 cm²
Perimeter 34 cm

Area 50 cm²
Perimeter 30 cm

f

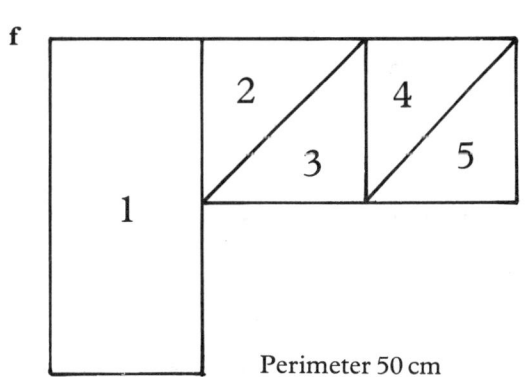

Perimeter 50 cm

g

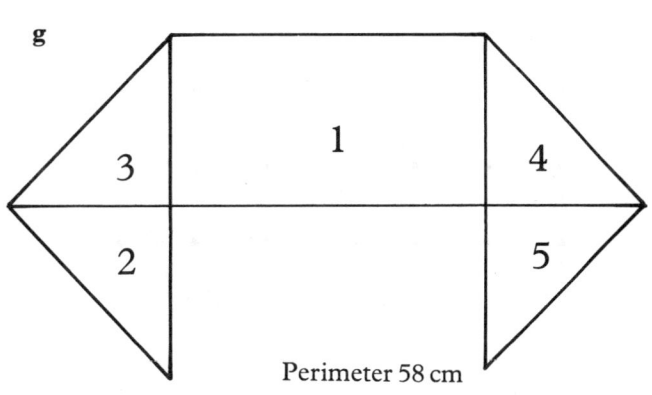

Perimeter 58 cm

Recording sheet for the 9-pin board

Recording sheet for the 16-pin board

Isometric grid

Longman Group UK Limited

Longman House,
Burnt Mill, Harlow,
Essex CM20 2JE, England
and Associated Companies
throughout the world.

© The Nuffield–Chelsea
Curriculum Trust 1989

First published 1989

Set in 10/12 point Plantin
(Lasercomp)
Produced by Longman Group
(F.E.) Limited
Printed in Hong Kong.

ISBN 0–582–02172–3